Called To The
Hard Places

Called To The Hard Places

Grace Chang

CHRISTIAN LITERATURE CRUSADE
Fort Washington, Pennsylvania 19034

CHRISTIAN LITERATURE CRUSADE

Box 1449, Fort Washington, PA 19034

ISBN 0-87508-093-6

PRINTED IN THE UNITED STATES OF AMERICA

CONTENTS

Edited by
Beryl Cullen
and
Robert Delancy

Chapter 1

In the Day of Trouble

It was December 8, 1941, in the little farm village of north China where I was serving the Lord. The sun was early in slipping behind the distant hills that evening, and with the coming darkness a new chill rode the wind in its blustering sweep down the almost barren slopes and across the plains. Frost crusted the ground and brief flurries of snow spun across the sleeping fields, giving hint of what was to come.

I turned my back on the driving bite of the gale that swept around the corner of the building. Wearily I unlocked the door to my little apartment in the basement of the church and stepped inside.

Until that moment I had not realized how exhausted I was, or how heavy my ankle-length fur coat and my bag of simple remedies for infections, colds, and the flu had become. This particular afternoon, a rash of minor illnesses among the children had kept me busy until darkness and the deepening cold drove me home.

I fumbled for a match to light the lamp on the small stand near the wall. Its feeble rays reflected off the bare bricks and cast shadows around much of the room.

I paused for a moment at the nearby narrow window, feeling the icy chill that seeped through the glass. There was no heat in the building. Few homes in our part of north China were heated. Most veteran missionaries of our area wore the heavily quilted trousers and long coats which the Chinese wore. We also kept these on inside the house, so we were quite comfortable, save for the extremities. The cold was stiffening my fingers and nibbling at my toes and the tips of my ears.

I built a fire in the stove to heat the porridge I would have for supper, then sat on the raised platform that protruded from the rear

1

wall and tucked my feet under me to get them off the icy floor. The long section of stovepipe that was built under the platform grew quite warm from the smoke of the wood fire that had cooked my porridge. Now, as I sat over it, I could feel the warmth. As I ate, some of my weariness fled.

The local elders had promised to build a house for me once the church building was finished, but they hadn't gotten around to it yet. And that bothered me. I didn't care that they had wanted to finish the church before starting on another project; but as the months had passed and nothing more was done, I had begun to fret.

It wasn't that I was not comfortable enough in my basement apartment. Actually, it was as large, as warm, and as well furnished as most of their homes, so I was not thinking solely of my own personal needs. More important to me than comfort was the fact that they had not kept their word. To go back on such a promise to one of God's servants was a sign of spiritual coldness.

I had planned my new home in my mind. It was to be simple, but with walls thick enough to provide insulation against the wind and the cold. There would be more windows than in the average Chinese home and a stove for heat. I had been living in China for twenty-two years but still had not grown accustomed to unheated homes. This was my plan for a house of my own, if it ever came to reality.

In most matters the elders were considerate of my every wish or desire—so I did not feel I could say anything to them about this, but I was *praying* about it, asking God to lay the matter on their hearts. I was soon to learn that their hesitation in building a house for me was part of God's plan.

I was reading my Bible half an hour or more later when I heard the scuffing of feet in the street outside the window. I was not alarmed. In all my years in China I had never been molested by bandits or thieves, and the people in the region were my friends. The Japanese had occupied our province for six years, but *they* had never bothered me either. Small wonder that I did not look up when I heard someone outside.

An instant later there was the harsh sound of shattering glass. I looked up, startled, to see a bayonet being forced through the window. For the first time since the early days of my arrival in China, I was frightened. I leaped to my feet, trembling.

At the time, because of my isolation from the outside world and my immersion in my work, I knew nothing about the attack on Pearl Harbor or the fact that our two countries were at war. Startled by the soldiers' sudden visit, I did as I was ordered and immediately unlocked the door. There was no time for me to put anything away before letting them in. No time to hide a thing.

That, I learned later, was the reason for the abrupt appearance of the officer and his armed escorts. The same tactics were being used against all the Americans and British who lived in other outlying villages. Japanese troops swooped down from the hills and rushed into the houses so quickly that no one had opportunity to squirrel anything away. They then scooped up personal papers, radios, and anything else that might even remotely indicate that the individual was in some way working against the Japanese government.

As the young officer entered my room he cried, "There is war! You are under arrest! By the order of the Emperor of Japan!"

I said nothing. I was too frightened to speak.

"Where do you live?" he demanded.

"Here," I stammered with a weak gesture.

He realized that it was the truth. His eyes told him that this was where I made my home. His sharp gaze picked out my porridge bowl and he saw that I ate the same simple food as did the people I served. This was bewildering to him. He expected Americans to live in Western-style houses and to eat Western food. Finding one who lived like an Oriental was disconcerting.

I was to learn months later that his report to his superiors described the church building as "beautiful." "But the foreigner is a pauper," he wrote. Because he thought I had nothing, he did not open the trunk or search the storeroom. Of course I didn't have anything that could have been construed as being subversive to the Japanese, but he could have confiscated the few things I did have and quickly taken me off to a concentration camp on nothing more than a personal whim.

This was God's reason for keeping me in the church basement! And I had been impatient with His people for being slow in carrying out their promise to build me a house. How penitent I was for my lack of trust!

With little more than a glance at me he strode to my desk, then piled everything from it onto the tablecloth and wrapped it up. He took every letter from home, every scrap of paper. Had I been carrying on any activity they thought harmful to them, they would have known it.

"Now come with me!" he ordered.

My fears increased. I knew about armies and the wave of rape and abuse and murder that so often followed them. I didn't want to go with him but I was alone. There was nothing else I could do. Wordlessly I got my coat and two blankets and followed him, praying for God's protection. I didn't know where he was taking me or what would happen when I got there. I didn't know how long I would be away or whether I would ever see the church again.

The officer mounted his horse, and with his squad of soldiers surrounding me I was marched off to his quarters in a nearby town. They unlocked the gate to the wall that surrounded the house where he lived, led me past the huge German shepherd that guarded the courtyard, and took me inside. What I feared most had come true. There was no one else in the room with us, and he was armed. He could do whatever he wished with me. There was no one to help me, except the Lord.

He ordered me to sit down. I was on one side of the low Japanese table and he was on the other. I was so badly frightened I was not sure I could reply when he interrogated me, but I tried hard to keep my captor from knowing it.

After the questioning he told me, "Go into the bedroom."

I could not read his intent, but my heart feared the worst.

"No," I retorted sharply. "I'll sleep out here."

To my surprise he did not insist, but went into the bedroom himself. "Oh, Lord," I prayed silently, "make me holy in his eyes."

I lay down on the floor, pulled the blanket over me and closed my eyes . . . but my body was rigid and my ears strained for every sound. At any moment I expected him to get to his feet and come for me.

I still did not know whether he was acting under orders or simply using the war as an excuse to take me. The Japanese were highly disciplined as soldiers, I reasoned. I had seen them often enough in the past six years to know that. It seemed logical that he was carrying out a command from his superiors.

But he was alone and I was a defenseless woman—a hated Westerner and a representative of the enemy. Would his superiors care what he did to me?

Chapter 2

"Unto All the World" Means China, Too

Lying there sleeplessly, my mind wandered back to the time when I received Christ as Savior. It had been in Massachusetts. I was a gangling, thin-faced little vixen with pigtails and a quick, mischievous smile, as fun-loving and exuberant as any eight-year-old. A few Sundays later I asked to be baptized, but the pastor refused, saying I was too young. The church board agreed with him. I repeated my request.

"It is encouraging that you want to be baptized, Grace." he told me gently, "but baptism is a very serious step and one that each person has to weigh carefully before taking it. Wait until you are old enough to understand exactly what you are doing."

"I understand *now*," I countered.

"Do you know how you are saved?" he persisted.

"By confessing the bad things I've done and asking Jesus to save me."

"By that do you mean that you are a sinner?"

I nodded.

"And why do you want to be baptized?"

"So people will know that I am a Christian," I said, after thinking awhile.

He continued to question me and finally had to conclude that I understood what it meant to be a Christian, so reluctantly he agreed to baptize me. Happy, I went bouncing out of his office.

The night I was baptized the congregation sang "Where He Leads

Me I Will Follow." "Can you say this from your heart, Grace?" the pastor asked seriously, when they had finished.

"Yes," I said without hesitation. I didn't know until years afterward why I was able to answer that question so quickly and with such firmness: before I was born Mother had dedicated me to Christ and had prayed that I would be a missionary.

For several years I attended Sunday School and church regularly and walked close with the Lord. Then in high school I drifted into the ways of my more worldly classmates. I learned to dance, and before long I was attending every dance I could manage to get to, although I was careful to keep Mother from finding out. She had firm convictions about separation from the world and laid down an edict to us. We were not to dance, go to the theater or movies.

She had always told us that such things would put a barrier between ourselves and the Lord. I soon discovered that it was true. I didn't want to go to church any more and began to resist Mother's efforts to get me there. At first she made me go, but as the tension increased between us, she stopped forcing me. Her concern did not cease, however, nor her efforts to bring me back under the influence of the church and solid Bible teaching.

About that time we moved to a new community, and Mother soon found a church home there.

"There's a girl who goes to my church that I'd like to have you meet," she would say. "She's a little older than you are—but I've never seen anyone so dedicated to the Lord." A wistful look crept into her eyes. It was always there when she talked about this Ella Finch, and I hated it—and her!

My contempt for Ella grew. "Mother's Little Angel," I called her. I was fifteen at the time and determined to go my own way and live my own life—which did not include going to church or living in an acceptable way for Mother and people like Ella. I had decided I was going to live my own life, without interference from anyone.

But Mother continued to talk about Ella and, I am sure, to pray for me. She must have had the entire church praying for me as well. Finally, in spite of myself, I began to grow curious. I began to wonder what this super-Christian was really like. What was there about her that would captivate Mother so much that she longed to have me to be just like her?

Though stubborn and rebellious, inwardly I longed for acceptance and approval. I wanted my mother and her friends to look on me with favor, in spite of my protests that I didn't care what anybody thought. So finally I relented and agreed to go to church with Mother again. I made it plain, however, that it was not going to become a habit. I was going once and only once.

"I'll be honest with you," I told her. "I really don't want to go to church, but I'll go tomorrow. I'm going because I want to see that 'angel' of yours."

Mother was so happy about it I almost changed my mind. I must be letting myself in for something, I reasoned, or she wouldn't be so pleased that I was going to go with her.

"There's one thing certain," I promised myself firmly. "I'm stuck this time, but I'll know better than to get myself in this kind of a bind again."

The meeting was held in a home, which only heightened my scorn for the whole affair. This could not be much of a church, I told myself. They didn't even have a decent place to hold their meetings. I went in with Mother, but instead of sitting with her near the front I found a seat in the last row. I sat there stiffly, looking straight ahead and determined to close my ears for the next hour or so.

I don't remember anything about the sermon. I had expected a fire-eating orator who thundered out his warnings in ungrammatical sentences like a prophet of doom, but the speaker wasn't like that. In fact, the message was quite ordinary. Ten minutes after it was over I couldn't have told anyone the text it was based on. And that was exactly the way I wanted it.

Ella Finch was there, as Mother had said she would be. I had been expecting a plain, unattractive person with solemn features and old-fashioned clothes, but I was surprised to see that she was as vivacious and gay as she was pretty. I felt myself drawn to her, instinctively. There was something about her smile that tugged at my heart.

If any of Mother's older friends had approached me about my spiritual need I would have stormed out of there before they finished talking. But I felt no resentment when at the close of the service Ella came and sat beside me.

In closing, the congregation had sung a song with the line, "Keep the oil in my lamp. . . ."

"You would like to change the words of that song, wouldn't you?" she ventured.

I eyed her curiously but said nothing.

"You would like to sing, *'Give* me oil in my lamp,' wouldn't you?"

I was astonished at her discernment. I didn't know that the sin of my life or the longing of my heart showed through so plainly.

"Yes," I said, so quickly and with such firmness that I was startled by it. "Yes, I would." Ella had such a warm, friendly manner I was not embarrassed to make such a confession to her. In fact, I was glad for the opportunity to talk to her.

We went over the matter of sin and dedication and walking with Christ in general terms, and finally we knelt to pray. I did not confess my sin aloud, but the Lord was speaking clearly to my heart. He brought to mind the things I was doing that were displeasing to Him. He put His finger on the sin of rebellion and the way I had turned my back on Him and the church. He made me see that my deceit was as sinful as dancing and that I had to get things straightened out between Mother and me. When I got to my feet I knew that I could not rest until I had confessed everything and asked for forgiveness.

Mother and I had a wonderful time that afternoon, praising God for the way He had worked in my life. Until that time I could not remember having such fellowship with her. Her joy that I had come back to Christ was soon replaced by concern for the future, however. She was looking beyond that day to the time when I would meet my former friends. She knew how difficult I would find it to walk in the way I should.

"Ella doesn't live close enough to spend much time with you, Grace," she said thoughtfully, "and I don't know of any other Christian girls in our neighborhood. Do you?"

I had to admit that I didn't.

"You have to have Christian fellowship," Mother went on.

She began to talk to me about going to Bible school. I was underage, but once I agreed to follow her suggestion she set out to find a school that would take me. I don't know how many Bible schools she contacted or how many refused me. The school in New Jersey may have been the first or the twenty-first. It really doesn't matter. The important thing is that they agreed to take me as a student. I only stayed three months, but that was long enough to ground me in my faith. When those three months were up I came home, got a job, and worked for a year.

Chapter 3

China?

I have forgotten exactly how God first spoke to me about China . . . but I know I didn't want to go. I was determined not to become a missionary, and even more determined not to go to China.

I have always envied those people who have heard God's claim on their lives, received Him as Savior, and then immediately knew His will and accepted it as the center of their lives. I have never been that way. God has had to deal patiently and sternly with me, showing me again and again what He would have me do. Even after I came back to Him and spent time in Bible school, I was not ready to accept His will for my life. I could give lip service to it. I could tell people I was praying for His guidance and asking Him to open the way for me to serve Him. In a way that was what I wanted. (At least I thought I did.) But I wanted to reserve a part for myself in making the final decision. I wanted God to show me what I should do and then allow *me* to say whether I wanted to or not. So God first had to bring me to the place where I was willing to accept His call to China *if* He would open the way for me. But that was just one step toward yielding my stubborn will. "Any place but China, Lord," was my real attitude.

The people at Mother's church in Springfield distressed me more than I would admit. She had shared my problem with them, the way I had presented it to her. They joined her in praying that God would open the way for me to serve Him in China. I couldn't even go to a youth meeting without hearing the leader voice that prayer. I suppose they thought I was thrilled to know their concern for me.

In desperation I quit going to that church and sought out an obscure little mission church uptown, a church where no one knew anything about me. But I reckoned without the long arm of God. He brought a woman to our service to give her testimony. Along with other things she mentioned was a loose quotation of Ecclesiastes 5:4. "When you vow a vow to God," she said, "be sure and pay it."

I recognized that God was speaking to me. The following Sunday I went back to my own church. Still, I was undecided.

Not long after, the Bible school I had attended had a special conference and I took time from my work and went down there. At one of the first meetings I knelt and turned complete control of my life over to the Lord. I thought I had done that long ago, but in the auditorium at Bible school I finally saw that I had been allowing myself to be blinded.

"You must settle it, God," I told Him. "If you want me to go to China, I will. If you want me to stay, I will stay. But I have to have the whole mess straightened out. I can't go on like this."

He gave me a scripture that evening as I knelt. John 15:16: "Ye have not chosen me, but I have chosen you, and ordained you that ye should go and bring forth fruit."

I could have twisted that verse to make myself believe it meant I could serve Him by witnessing at a hospital somewhere (I had wanted to become a dietician) but I *knew* that wasn't what He meant. Before I got to my feet the matter was settled. I could not argue any more. I had to yield to His leading. He knew my abilities and my circumstances. He knew all about me.

The decision was all my own. Nobody at the conference was expecting anything of me. When I got home, however, an elderly black lady came up and put a dollar bill in my hand. "This is for China," she said. "The Lord is calling. He told me to give it to you." That was a great encouragement to me.

Once my future was resolved, I quit my job, enrolled in Bible School once more, and stayed on in New Jersey until I graduated three years later. I had fought bitterly against the Lord's call to be a missionary, but once I yielded to His will I was determined to get out to China as quickly as possible.

It was after I had decided to go to the mission field that I learned the Lord had been dealing with Ella Finch as well. She too was going to be a missionary in China. Although we didn't know it at that time, we would be going out to the field together—Ella to the south and I to one of the northern provinces.

Going out as a missionary in the early 1900's was different than it is today. It was not uncommon to go out independently, which is the way I went. I didn't have to concern myself with applying to a mission and satisfying a board that I could meet certain spiritual, educational and physical requirements. In those days we felt a call, got the education we thought necessary, contacted churches for support, and booked passage. The system we have today results in better-qualified missionaries, but our way was much simpler.

Everyone said I was like my mother when it came to setting my heart on a course of action and sticking with it. Mother had been brought up in one of the wealthiest families in Ireland. Everyone had expected her to find a husband among her own set. But she fell in love with a sailor, who later became a Salvation Army officer. Mother defied an ultimatum that she would be disinherited, trained as an Army officer and followed my father to Canada. Later they were married and moved to the U.S.

Many times I have thanked God for that streak of stubborn iron will I inherited from my mother. Firmly disciplined by the Holy Spirit, it often gave me the strength to keep going when I really wanted to quit.

Although Mother knew I was as single-minded and as obstinate as she was, she still feared for me when the time came for me to think seriously about leaving home.

"You can't go with so little money, Grace," she protested. "You don't have the clothes and other things you will need. You don't have a train ticket to Seattle or the money to pay your fare to China by boat."

I knew that everything she said was true, but I was young and inexperienced and flushed with the elation of being chosen to serve God. I could talk glibly about being willing to make any sacrifice God asked me to make, but I didn't really know what I was saying. Secretly, I guess I welcomed the prospect of privation as a means of showing my devotion to God. There was spiritual pride in my attitude. I wanted people to look at me and marvel at the way I loved God; I wanted to be singled out as a spiritual giant. However, I soon learned great things about His keeping power and the way He takes care of His own, and my pride began to evaporate.

Two days after Mother telling me I couldn't leave for China as planned because I didn't have money for clothes and supplies or tickets, I received a phone call from a wealthy man in our community. He told me that he had some things in his attic I could have if I wished.

Among them were five pairs of ladies' shoes that fit me perfectly.

My friends at the office also began to give me things, and by the following Friday I had three trunks jammed to capacity. One contained a sewing machine and a typewriter.

"And Mother," I exclaimed in jubilation, "they are so full the express man had to sit on them to help me get them closed!"

She was grateful for the way God had supplied. She was also pleased, I know, that I was putting my love for God ahead of my concern for myself, and that I was going ahead with my plans to serve Him. She had been praying for that to happen since before I was born. Still, her mother's love wouldn't quite allow her to place me completely and unconditionally in God's care.

"You still don't have any money," she reminded me. "And you will have to have money if you are going to get out to China."

I knew that, but I was not concerned. Trusting God was exciting. I could scarcely wait to see what He was going to do for me next.

It was inevitable that Ella Finch and I became very good friends. After I yielded to Christ's call and learned that she was also going to China, a bond was forged between us. It soon became apparent that it would be wise for us to go out together. Having Ella with me also made Mother feel better about my leaving with so little money. Somehow she felt that two of us could get along better in a difficult situation than one. Both Ella and I were glad to have the opportunity to travel together.

* * * * *

When we left Massachusetts in 1919 for the West Coast and the ship that would take us to our mission field, our spirits were soaring. We spoke in various churches along the way and got enough money from them to travel from one city to the next—until we reached Chicago.

"I don't have enough money to get to the church where I'm supposed to speak tonight," I confided to Ella.

I needn't have been disturbed, for God knew all about it and had already undertaken for us. When I checked at the forwarding address I had given before leaving home, I discovered a letter from Mother. She had enclosed a check that had come for me from my aunt in England. God had spoken to her heart weeks before and guided that letter to reach me at exactly the moment when my need was the greatest!

I cried. I could not help it.

I usually warn young missionaries about planning ways for God to supply their needs. "You don't have to build God a railroad to your door for Him to take care of you," I say. "Share your needs with Him and leave them there. Trust Him to supply without your help or suggestions."

We finally got to Seattle and were leaving the next day for Vancouver, British Columbia, with just enough money to get us there. It was Wednesday night and both Ella and I wanted to go to prayer meeting, so we chose the church nearest the place where we were staying. We must have looked like missionaries because the pastor came up and asked if we were. He had us give our testimonies during the service, and when we finished he told the people that he was not going to take up an offering for us, "but if any of you feel led to give the girls anything as you go out, I would urge you to do so."

We didn't expect anything. Actually, we had not gone to the service expecting money. Still, we received that night the largest offering of any on our trip across the country. It was proof that God was taking care of us.

At a Bible Conference the previous summer I had met a veteran missionary from China who was home on furlough and was going back about the time Ella and I planned to sail. Hopefully I asked her if we could go out to China with her—but we received little encouragement. If anything, she acted as though she would just as soon not be bothered with us.

"If you're ready," she told us, "you can go on the same boat I have passage on, provided there is space." She made us understand that she was not going to wait on us nor make any unusual effort to help us.

Knowing we might be short of funds, she did write that she would arrange for us to stay in a private home for the few days we would be in Vancouver before shipping out. We counted on that, but when we got there we learned that there had been a mix-up of some sort and there was no private home available for us. We had to go to the Y.W.C.A. for a room.

"If we hadn't visited that church last night," Ella said gratefully, "we wouldn't have had enough money to pay for our room."

Chapter 4

A Stranger in a Strange Land

Ella and I boarded the ship shortly after noon, got settled in our cabin, and later went on deck to watch the passing landscape as the ship crept slowly down the passageway in the direction of the open sea. The great pines and cedars along the rocky shores looked arrogantly down on the occasional puny hardwood whose brilliant cloak would soon be snatched away, leaving it naked and shivering until spring. I glanced at Ella who was standing beside me at the railing.

"I wonder what we will be doing at this time next year," I said thoughtfully.

There was a distant look in her eyes, but she didn't reply.

"It's going to be hard learning the language and getting used to Chinese food."

She nodded wordlessly.

I was silent for a moment. We hadn't said much to each other since leaving Vancouver. It was unusual for us not to talk. When we were together we usually chattered as excitedly as any other nineteen- or twenty-year-olds. Only right then we didn't feel a great deal like talking. My thoughts drifted back across the water to the great landmass that was America. I wondered about our families—how long it would be until we saw them and our beloved New England again.

I glanced at my watch. It was three-thirty. "I suppose my mother is getting ready to go to prayer meeting about now," I said.

She nodded. "Do you suppose they'll be praying for us?"

"I'm sure they will."

Time passed, while our ship churned cautiously down the inland waterway on her journey to the Pacific. Darkness tiptoed in. From our stern, as we passed Victoria, ten thousand lights winked at us, as though to wave goodbye.

In 1919, myriads of city lights were not common and the twinkling of a city after sunset fascinated me. I had often stood at the window in Boston, looking out over the fairyland of lights. All the sordidness and dirt of the city was hidden in the Christmas-like display, and I was entranced by it. But not that night. There was a sadness about the city glitter that I had difficulty in understanding.

"Isn't it beautiful, Ella?" I asked quietly. "Victoria, I mean."

"I wonder if Shanghai and Peking will be so sparkling and lovely?" she asked.

With a start I realized that I didn't even know if they had electricity in China.

I had much to learn and I suddenly realized that I was cutting myself off from the security of family, friends, and familiar places—and from the spiritual strength of my mother. I would no longer be able to go to her for counsel and guidance. Already I was feeling the nagging hurt of loneliness.

I glanced over at Ella and the knot in my stomach tightened. Everyone had told me how wonderful it was to serve God—how it provided the only means of true happiness. At that time I could not see much pleasure in the heartache I was experiencing. Was this what it was like to be a missionary?

It was not that our resolve wavered, nor our determination to serve Christ on a mission field where customs were as different to ours as the language of the people, and just as difficult to understand. Both Ella and I were excited about going to China, but there had been a strange ethereal quality about the months preceding our departure as we applied for our passports, got innoculations and visas, and talked eagerly of the day when we would leave. Yes, there had been a vapid, dream-like quality in our plans, like the times when we played house as girls. We would enter into our elaborate charades—but when our mothers called us we stepped blithely out of our make-believe world into the familiar world of home. Now, that was no longer possible. We were going thousands of miles from home and would be staying for years. We were not sure when we would be coming back on furlough, or what would happen to us in China.

I tried to talk to Ella again but she spoke only in response to a direct question. She didn't say it, but I knew that she shared the agony I was experiencing. Vainly I tried to shake it away.

The older missionary, Mabel Steiner, joined us about that time. She stood quietly beside Ella, staring with us out over the placid strait. She sensed our uneasiness and the reasons for it.

"It's always like this when you first leave," she said.

My cheeks flushed and I looked away, embarrassed that she knew my heart.

"Will it ever get any better?" Ella asked.

Mabel nodded. "You'll feel differently in the morning."

I didn't see why that would be, but I did not challenge her statement.

"It hurts terribly now," she repeated with understanding that surprised me. "But when we're out at sea tomorrow you'll be better—"

"By morning," I thought, "we will be farther from home than ever, and that will only make things worse."

"—if you're not too seasick to care," Mabel added.

We went to bed at the usual hour. I didn't think it was any use, that I would not sleep at all, but I did. I hadn't realized how exhausted I was until my head hit the pillow. I suppose much of my weariness was brought on by tension. When we wakened the next morning, however, I was surprised at how well I felt.

"Everyone has been telling us how we would begin to miss meals once we got out to sea," I announced proudly to the people at our breakfast table, "but I don't think I'm going to be seasick. In fact, I feel wonderful."

"So do I," Ella added.

There were no experienced travelers among us, so we were all congratulating ourselves on our seaworthiness when I chanced to look up. An oval of not blue but green was visible through the nearest porthole.

"Look, girls!" I cried so loudly the passengers at every table in the dining salon stared at us. "There's land! We haven't sailed yet!"

"That can't be!" Ella exclaimed. However, it was true.

We were secured to a dock at Port Angeles, Washington, and hundreds of Chinese men in their traditional work clothes were filing aboard. Because they were Chinese, I was interested instantly. I felt an almost proprietary sense of responsibility for them. And what was happening to them was suddenly of grave concern to me.

"Who are those men?" I asked our steward when he came to our table with more coffee.

He knew who I was talking about without looking up.

"Just some coolies we're taking back to China," he explained. "They worked in France during the war, but now that's over and they aren't needed any longer, so we're taking them home."

"All of them?" It seemed incredible that there was room for so many, even though our ship looked huge to me.

"All two thousand of them," he retorted indifferently.

I looked around. The salon was full and I was sure that every cabin in the ship had already been filled. "But—" I began.

"You don't have to worry," the steward continued, misunderstanding my concern. "They won't be up here. They'll be in steerage." He gestured expressively. "Below."

I shuddered. I had heard all sorts of stories about steerage. I could see two thousand men crowded into quarters so small they would scarcely have room to lie down, with food ladled to them from big black kettles once a day. I was about to explode to the steward but realized that would accomplish nothing. He was as helpless to change the situation as I was.

* * * * *

Eighteen days later, when we had finally crossed the Pacific, we stopped at the first port in China to unload the men in steerage before going on to Shanghai, my immediate destination. Ella and I stood on deck and watched the men file up the gangplank past the British officer with a counter in his hand. He was checking to be sure the right number was there.

"Like so many cattle," I murmured. At the age of nineteen I was short on understanding and quick to be outraged at real and fancied injustices.

"And look! They're loading them into cattle cars! Those poor men! It's positively inhuman!"

Ella was going to stay on board ship longer than I, for she was going to a mission station some distance to the south. But I was headed for Tientsin. In port at Shanghai, Ella and I said good-by, tearfully. We had known since we left Boston that this time of parting would come. I felt called to the North and Ella was interested in going to the South. Yet, now that the time for parting had come, we were naturally upset.

In a way I felt more helpless and alone at the thought of leaving Ella than I had at leaving Mother. We had faced so many unknown situations since leaving home that we had come to depend upon each other. Now I would not have Ella with me. I had to face a strange land alone.

I disembarked and waited for my trunks to be brought ashore by the line of coolie stevedores. I was almost overwhelmed by the seething jumble of humanity. I had been in Boston and New York and Philadelphia many times, but even in the busiest rush hours I had never seen such crowds.

The nearby fish market was a surging mass of people, fighting their way from one stall to another, buying the prawns, squid, or fish they needed for the meals of the day. An old man moved past me in the queer, swinging half-trot I was soon to become accustomed to. He had a long pole on his shoulder, carrying a heavily ladened basket on either end. A pregnant woman tottered past me on her pitifully bound feet, a dozing baby on her back. And everywhere there was the unintelligible rumble of voices. I wondered if I would ever be able to master their tongue.

Mabel approached me, "Oh, there you are. I wondered what happened to you."

My smile was frozen and lifeless. I don't remember what I said, but it wasn't important.

She got a rickshaw for me and told the man to load my trunks.

"Are you sure you don't want to go to the guest house where they're expecting you?"

"Positive."

I had written ahead for a room, but I had been told afterward that the people there did everything they could to keep new missionaries in Shanghai. That was not for me. I was like a swallow in the spring pointing her bill northward. God had given me a destination and I *had* to go there.

"All right. I'll have him take you to another Christian guest house."

I got into the rickshaw and the coolie put himself between the shafts. It was disturbing to me to sit while another person pulled me around. I would much rather have walked beside him. Only I could not have kept up with that rhythmic trot of his. His pace seemed effortless, as if he could go on for hours without faltering.

I leaned back and stared at the scene. The city was unlike any I had ever seen. The buildings were narrow, two-story structures with shops below and living quarters above. Then there were the shacks of the poor, built of lumber and scrap materials. And the people! Everywhere there were people: great churning masses of them.

Then I noticed the bars on the windows and waves of fear swept over me. Stories I had heard about the white slave trade in the Orient rushed to mind. I recalled tales of girls being snatched off the streets and pressed into prostitution. It could happen to me, I decided, and nobody at home would ever know what had happened to me.

In that sea of Oriental faces I saw one that was European. In desperation, I made the rickshaw boy understand that I wanted to stop. I leaped from the rickshaw, rushed over to the tall European and blurted out my problem. I didn't know where I was going. The rickshaw boy could have been taking me wherever he wanted to and I would never have known the difference—until it was too late.

"You're not too far away now," the stranger said, pointing to a building up the street two- or three-hundred yards.

I was so grateful I could have kissed him! And the rickshaw boy as well. He was actually taking me where I wanted to go!

At the guest house I made the rickshaw boy understand that I wanted my bags carried in. After I had been in China for a time I learned that a Westerner struggled with his bags alone, no matter how heavy they were. If a coolie got into the house it was very difficult to get him out.

I had another problem I didn't know I had. I was arriving at the guest house unannounced and without a reservation, I knew, but strangely they did not seem surprised to see me.

"We're so happy to have you with us," I was told. "We have your room ready for you."

My eyes widened. Since leaving home I had often been astonished by the way the Lord worked. "I haven't booked a room," I said.

The hostess faced me incredulously. "Who are you, anyway?"

"Grace Kenning."

"And you didn't write for a room?" she asked, as though there had to be some mistake.

"Not here. I decided to come and stay with you after talking with some people on the boat." I read the dismay in her face. "It's all right, isn't it?"

"It would be, except that we don't have any space," she blurted. "The only room we have empty is reserved for a missionary from the next province who's due to arrive here any time."

I was ready to cry.

"I—I just got off the boat from America," I stammered miserably, "and I don't have much money. I must have a place to stay."

Then one of the guests volunteered to take me in with her. I thanked her profusely. That room looked like the presidential suite to me.

Her smile was warm and pleasant. "Think nothing of it, my dear. I remember how I felt when I first came out. I'd sleep in the hall before I'd let you leave here with no place to go."

I wanted to throw my arms about her neck and kiss her, but she looked a bit too prim and austere for that.

I had managed to bring some money with me from America. At the rate of exchange I expected to get I figured on having enough to pay my train fare to Tientsin and still have enough left over for my first month or two. However when I went to the bank, my American dollars only bought half the Chinese dollars I thought they would. I had enough to pay for my ticket from Shanghai to Tientsin. That was all.

The next few days were a jumble of strange sights and sounds and smells as I walked the streets of Shanghai with one of the other missionaries, as though in a dream. I wondered if I would ever be able to do anything for the Lord now that I was here.

Then the time came for me to leave the city and I was loaded into one of those windowless cars I had thought were so terrible for the coolies. I was on my way to Tientsin, and the Clarks, a couple who were with the China Inland Mission, were going part of the way with me.

The car was not unlike the boxcars we used in the States for hauling livestock, except that the sides were boarded solid. It was unheated and fairly dark, and was already filling with people who had crowded ahead of us.

I looked around, blinking against the deep shadows. When my eyes were accustomed to the semi-darkness I saw that long benches, back to back, ran down the spine of the car, with space on either side for baggage.

Few of the passengers, save the handful of foreigners, had suitcases. But that had not stopped the others from bringing their possessions aboard. There were boxes and sacks and crates of vegetables and rice and chickens and ducks. An overpowering stench went up from the poultry and fish and decaying vegetables.

My nostrils pinched shut and nausea swept over me. For an instant I was sure that I was going to be sick. I shook off my weakness and marched to a bench where I sat down next to a Chinese man. I gave myself a little space to move, but that didn't last long. People shoved me over until I was jammed against him on one side and Mrs. Clark on the other. I could breathe, but moving was almost impossible.

I glanced over at the man sitting beside me. He was wearing a quilted jacket and trousers, and homemade shoes with layer on layer of some substance that looked like paper, for soles.

He seemed oblivious to the fact that there was anyone close to him and completely insensitive to my revulsion at the way he was constantly spitting on the floor around him. I shuddered every time it happened and tried to draw farther away, but we were like so many grains of rice in a bag. I could not put any space between us. Briefly the nausea rushed back.

Mrs. Clark saw my predicament and volunteered to trade places with me. I studied her gentle features curiously. She was no more insensitive than I.

"Thank you," I said with an air of martyrdom, "but I can't do that. It's no more pleasant for you than it is for me."

"But I'm used to it," she countered. "And after you've been here a while you'll get used to it, too."

I didn't contradict her openly but at that moment I didn't believe I would ever get used to these sights and smells! Gratefully, I traded places with her.

She was right, of course. The time was to come when I, too, would be able to block out of my consciousness little matters like someone coughing in my face or spitting on the floor around my feet.

When we reached the next station, tradesmen swarmed aboard selling hard-boiled eggs, still steaming from the boiling water. The Chinese around us bought them, holding them gingerly in their dirty hands. Streams of black water coursed down their fingers. I shuddered and looked away as the man beside me cracked an egg and noisily began to eat.

"Are you hungry?" my friend asked me. "Would you like something to eat, too?"

"No, thank you." I fought the churning in my stomach. "I don't think I can *ever* eat again."

She smiled in silence. I was young and a stranger to China. I had to have time to get used to it.

Chapter 5

A Place to Serve

When we finally reached Tientsin I got off the train, anxiously searching the crowd for the familiar face of Agnes Carmichael. Although Agnes was at least twice my age, she too was in her first term as a missionary. I had known her in Bible school where she had been two classes ahead of me.

We weren't close friends, but we did know each other—and when she had written inviting me to come and help her, I was ecstatic. I was sure it was the leading of the Lord.

But where was she? And how would I be able to find her if she did not come to the station? I was almost out of money and could neither write nor speak the language. Panic seized me in its icy fingers. What was I going to do?

And then I saw her standing to one side, a little apart from the crowd, as though she wanted to make sure that I would see her. She towered above the diminutive Chinese, a head taller than anyone else in the crowd. I breathed a prayer of thanksgiving that she had come to meet me.

"I'm so glad to see you, Grace," Agnes said as I approached her. "One of the men came with me to handle your luggage and drive the cart." And then, so I would not get the wrong impression, she added quickly, "He's one of the *married* missionaries."

The two-wheeled cart was scarcely large enough for my trunks and the three of us. Mr. Martin sat with his feet over the edge of the cart and I was squeezed in next to him. My legs were turned back and squashed under me.

I didn't know how long the ride took, but my legs were throbbing painfully even before the skinny little horse began to move the creaking cart over the trail toward our village. But I didn't say anything.

I was a missionary. Missionaries didn't complain; they suffered in silence. At the same time I had the mistaken idea that there was some virtue in physical suffering. I reasoned that I would be a better servant of God if I endured the ordeal of riding on my legs, in spite of the pain. The more they hurt, the better missionary I would be.

I soon discovered that, in spite of the fact that God had called me to the mission field, I was still very human—with all the needs and hurts experienced by others. When I went without food I got hungry. When I bumped myself, it hurt. I learned that there was no particular merit in needless suffering. In fact, I decided that such self-torture was not pleasing to God. When suffering was forced upon us because of our faith, that was, however, an entirely different matter.

Some two hours later, when we finally reached our destination, I had great difficulty in crawling out of the cart. I could scarcely hobble after Agnes through the gate. It was some time before the pain subsided enough so I could take in my surroundings.

I was glad to find that Agnes was living in a house built exactly like the others in the village. I was very anxious to live like the Chinese.

A brick wall was at the front, and with it three small buildings formed a square around a courtyard. There was one main house and two smaller ones for servants and guests. The roofs were thatched and the narrow windows all faced inward onto the courtyard. Somehow the walled courtyard and the absence of outward-facing windows symbolized for me the barriers of Buddhism and ancestor worship that faced us.

Back in Shanghai I had been surprised when I discovered that the guest house used linen and silverware on the tables. Although I had been given tablecloths and napkins and had brought them with me at Mother's insistence, I figured that missionaries would be living on such an elevated spiritual plane they would not want such evidences of materialism around.

In the village where I was going I expected to be eating off a rough-hewn table with tin knives and forks and spoons. I could even envision tin plates. I was polishing my badge of martyrdom at every opportunity.

When I was called to dinner my first night in the house I stopped just inside the door, my eyes rounding in amazement. I had once visited my grandmother's home in Ireland, and as I now stared at the white table cloth and china and silver—which was really quite ordinary, now that I think back—all I could compare it to was the mansion in Ireland where my grandmother lived.

Agnes read my surprise and was annoyed by it. "Is there something wrong?" she asked.

"No," I answered, "there's nothing wrong. Only— " How could I tell her I had come prepared to eat rice with chopsticks out of a chipped bowl?

She knew what I was thinking.

"Just because we're missionaries," she informed me, "doesn't mean that we have to live differently than we do at home. I happen to enjoy my food more when it's served this way, and I'm sure you will, too."

That ended the discussion. We went in to the table and sat down.

"The first thing you will have to do is learn the language." she told me as we finished dessert. "I've made arrangements for a tutor for you. You will start your lessons in Mandarin tomorrow morning."

That was good news for me. I was so anxious to start sharing Christ I would have taken my first language lesson that night if it had been possible. But there was something about the tone of her voice that disturbed me. I could not have explained the reason for my uneasiness. Yet, it was there. My gaze found hers and held it.

"Is it—is it hard, Agnes?" I stammered. It was not that I was afraid to tackle something difficult. I had my mother's disregard for obstacles. However, if learning the language was hard, it would take longer for me to learn to talk to the people about Christ.

She did not answer me immediately. She was looking back, to the time when she was first learning the language.

"Hard?" she echoed, the corners of her mouth tightening. "It was so hard I thought I would never master it." Just thinking about the problems she had in learning Mandarin caused her lips to tremble. "I cried so much those days I wet a hand towel with my tears." She paused, studying my face as though she read disbelief in it. "You'll find that it is the most difficult thing you have ever done."

Agnes had told me the truth about the language. It *was* hard to learn. In fact I soon discovered that it was the most arduous subject I had ever attempted. If I had had any lesser reason for wanting to learn Mandarin than my determination to help bring Jesus Christ to the

Chinese, I might have become discouraged and quit.

I studied six hours a day, six days a week. There were times when I felt like crying until *my* tears wet a hand towel, but I didn't. Not over learning Mandarin. There were other occasions when I did cry in bitterness and frustration and disappointment, but that was months later.

However, before the winter was over I was able to give my first testimony in Chinese. What an occasion that was! I didn't sleep much the night before, going over exactly what I was going to say. I savored each word, trying the pronunciation, working for exactly the right inflection. I prayed that some heart might be touched by my first efforts.

"I'm frightened, Agnes," I said at the breakfast table that morning.

Her slender fingers encircled her tea cup, thoughtfully. "I'm sure you are, but you have to start sometime."

The meeting I spoke at was supposed to be for women only, but a large crowd of both men and women pressed to come in. One of the women in charge came to me in some consternation and asked what they should do.

"Let them come in," I said, exulting to think that they were clamoring to hear the gospel. "By all means. Let them come in!" As I saw it, God was giving us a unique opportunity to serve Him.

When I got up to speak and looked out over those curious faces, reason left me and for one terrifying moment I forgot everything I was going to say. But I could not disappoint them. I opened my mouth and began to speak.

At first the words came haltingly, with long pauses between. Then I began to feel the excitement of my first opportunity to share Christ in Chinese. I began to speak faster and faster, stumbling over my carefully prepared words. Before I was half finished, I was speaking in a horrible conglomeration of Chinese, English, and high-school German. I was so thrilled at the opportunity to say something that I was speaking in one unintelligible flood of words. In spite of that, my first testimony before a Chinese audience was the most exciting thing that had happened to me since I had left home.

At home that evening I talked with Agnes about what had happened. I was sorry that she had not been there to see the crowd for herself. "I really made a mess of speaking," I admitted, "but the way they came and listened shows that they were anxious to hear the gospel," I told Agnes excitedly.

"Not necessarily." She had already had a full report of the afternoon meeting. "You had just as well know it, Grace. They didn't come to hear about Christ. You are something of an oddity here. They came to see your white skin and pink cheeks."

Like staring at a monkey in a zoo! I was crushed.

"That can't be!" I protested.

"Ask the pastor. He'll tell you. The people aren't as easy to reach with the gospel as that." She went on to explain some of the difficulties she and others had had. As much as I wanted to deny it, I knew that she was speaking the truth.

Again that night I cried. Why couldn't we see someone who was truly interested in receiving Christ as his Savior? Why did our ministry have to be so fruitless and discouraging? Briefly I wondered whether God had ever wanted me to serve Him in China. Perhaps my call to this harsh land had been *my* doing. Perhaps He didn't want me here at all! If He did, wouldn't He have blessed our ministry more openly?

As the years passed I began to see that God didn't use the same measuring device we use and that frequently a loyal, faithful servant would work for years without seeing visible results. This was another lesson the Lord had me learn early in my ministry. I suppose it was one of the hardest I had to understand.

* * * * *

Agnes was twenty years older than I, and having been on the field longer than I she did her best to establish a mother–daughter relationship between us. She told me in explicit detail everything that I was to do. I was expected to eat what she said I should, wear what she told me to, and arrange my schedule in the way she determined.

When we went to the stores in the city where we did our shopping, she would choose the food, according to her tastes. And they were quite unusual for a missionary. As governess in several wealthy American homes before going to Bible school she had learned to like expensive foods, and particularly rich desserts. I had been brought up on soups and puddings and had never eaten enough pie and cake to acquire a taste for them. However, I was expected to pay my half of the bill and to eat as she did. She didn't like it when I protested or left food, half-eaten, on my plate.

"Eat it, Grace," she would tell me softly when there were no Chinese close enough to overhear. "We can't leave any Western food for our servants. They will start eating it and it will spoil them when they leave us. They'll feel they have to eat the way we do and they won't be able to."

Those months with my co-worker were difficult for me. Rich food did not agree with me and I would get sick and lose one or two meals a week.

There were other difficulties as well. For one thing, I wanted to learn to *write* the Chinese language, but she decided that I wouldn't need it. "You will have enough trouble learning to speak and read Mandarin," she told me. "Besides, you won't have any need for writing. You can hire professional scribes to write your letters." She spoke with a finality that closed the subject.

I deferred to her edict but was sorry later.

I was far more disturbed by the way Agnes ordered me about than I would admit to myself. When she came to me with demands that seemed unreasonable my stomach would knot and pain would tear at me. Any sudden emotional change, either joy or sorrow, was enough to cause me to lose a meal, and I would feel terrible stomach pains.

My time with Agnes was the most difficult I had in all my years on the mission field. I had to keep telling myself that I was where I was because God had placed me there, and He placed me there because He had something He wanted me to learn from that experience. I used to throw myself across my bed and sob out my frustrations.

The source of much of my trouble was the idealistic view I had of missions and missionaries. I had thought that everything would be close to perfect once I was in China. Our lives would be ordered and simple with never any problems between myself and fellow missionaries. I firmly believed that God had made missionaries a group apart. We were all supposed to be even-tempered and forgiving and kind, never impatient or out of sorts, especially with each other. I had envisioned the mission field as a little oasis of perfection in an alien, unfriendly world.

This was far from reality. Again and again I saw the human side of God's servants and began to realize that He did not make us perfect— nor did He remove all the abrasiveness and selfishness from us the moment we decided to go out to the mission field. Our humanness caused all sorts of difficulties; in fact we had more problems on the field than we had at home.

I discovered that even as a missionary I had to work at living the Christian life, and work hard. I had to develop love and understanding and forgiveness. Those things were not automatically bestowed upon us. I used to cry out to God through my tears for guidance and strength, "Keep me in the center of Your will." Nothing has seemed hard to me since.

* * * * *

The members of our Chinese church would take me along when they went to share Christ with the people. I was not aware of it at the time, but I was the big attraction. Like the first gorilla in captivity that was on display with Ringling Brothers, Barnum & Bailey, I was the bait to draw a crowd and hold them. The Chinese would do the preaching.

They would have me stand on the steps of a little shop in the village while people came to look at my white face, my big nose and clumsy feet. As I became more proficient in the language I began to understand what they were saying.

"Did you ever see anyone with such a big nose?"

"And look at those feet." They clucked their sympathy for me. "Her father should have bound them."

As I grew to understand their comments I could also guess what they were thinking: The family of such a strange-looking girl would have difficulty in arranging any sort of marriage for her.

Some of the little girls who came to look at me would turn and run if I chanced to glance at them. This didn't help my self-confidence.

I was playing the organ in the church one Sunday morning when everyone in the audience started to laugh. I couldn't figure out what was going on until I spied a small boy who had just come in. Using charcoal he had blackened lines on his face to look like my heavy horn-rimmed glasses. He had already shown his artistic endeavor to the people in the back of the church. When I saw him, he was on his way forward to show those who were seated down front.

When he went out, with everyone laughing hysterically, I knew that he would be back. He had an audience. There had to be an encore.

Sure enough! In a few moments he returned. This time I was ready for him. As he came down the aisle I jumped off the platform and made a dive for him. He eluded my grasp and got away, but did not disrupt the service any more.

As I learned more of the language I was asked to speak more often, but it was not until I had served in China for a full term that I felt at ease with the difficult Mandarin tongue.

Chapter 6

With God's Help

Before my arrival in China, Agnes Carmichael had started an orphanage in a second village some distance from where we were living and set up a school so the children could be educated. A year or so after I went to work with her, we moved to that second village and I was put to work in the school.

Most of the thirty-five or forty children in the orphanage were girls, and in those days the Chinese didn't waste money on schools for girls. Many families simply threw the girl babies out, or if they showed promise of being attractive, kept them to sell later to some wealthy merchant.

There were Chinese teachers for most subjects, but as soon as I learned a few words of Mandarin I was given the responsibility of teaching the Bible lessons. Working with the children was delightful. They seemed to understand my pitiful Chinese better than the adults. They were more tolerant of my efforts and never seemed to tire of helping me. They would go over the pronunciation of words and phrases tirelessly, giggling in the universal language of children.

"No, no, no!" they would tell me, delightedly. "This is how you say it . . . ."

And when I finally mastered what I was trying to say, they were happier than I was.

One day they came to me about school uniforms. Each school had it's own special uniform that the students were expected to wear.

"All except ours," the delegation told me. "We wear anything we happen to have and it looks terrible. No one would even *know* that we are a school."

I had seen the children who attended the government-operated classes in other villages so I knew how important uniforms were to such youngsters. I had to admit they did look nice.

"But—" I began. Our children had no parents to pay for their uniforms and we certainly could not afford to have special clothes made for them. We were finding it difficult to pay our Chinese teachers and get supplies. There was no money to buy uniforms.

They seemed to know what I was thinking.

"You could make them for us, Miss Kenning, couldn't you?" one little girl pleaded. "We'll all help."

I was never able to resist children. Impulsively I put my arms around her and drew her close. "I can't make any promises," I said, "but we'll see."

They went skipping off, to spread the word that the school was soon going to have uniforms like all the others.

I didn't know what Agnes would think of it. At supper the entire orphanage buzzed with the news and as soon as the meal was over I went, with a certain hesitance, to talk to her about it.

"Do you think you can sew forty uniforms?" she asked me.

I had done a little sewing when I was a girl, but forty uniforms! That was something else. And I had never even made one.

I was about to admit the job was too great for me when I thought of my mother and her determination to do whatever she set her mind to.

"If you can get the material," I told her, "I'll make them."

Agnes loved the children as much as I did. From somewhere she got the money for the material and I set to work.

Had we been in the States my first move would have been to buy a series of patterns and work from them. However, patterns were not available in China. Someone brought me a sample of a very small jacket to serve as model. I was appalled to see that there were thirteen pieces neatly fitted together. It reminded me more of a jigsaw puzzle than a coat.

"Dear God," I prayed inwardly, "You're going to have to help me!"

Ripping the seams of my model and using the pieces as a guide, I cut out several jackets and fitted them to my eager subjects. The girls were ecstatic.

"We're going to have the most beautiful jackets in the whole world!" one of them said proudly, turning for the others to see.

I was pleased at her confidence, but still apprehensive. Pushing aside my own concern I began to sew. The task I feared so much did not prove to be all that difficult. By the time I had finished the first two or three, I was able to work smoothly and without problems. With the entire school watching my progress, their excitement growing, I sewed one jacket after another.

There was also the problem of shoes to go with the uniforms. No one had said anything to me about that until the jacket and skirt project was nearing completion. Then the new concern surfaced. What were they going to do for shoes to go with their magnificent new outfits?

It wasn't as if they were asking me for leather shoes. They wore shoes that were traditional for our area, with cloth uppers and soles made of layers of heavier cloth glued together and sewed with heavy thread.

When I finished the jackets I made the tops of the shoes on my hand machine. The Christian women in the village made the soles. It was a huge job, but they too wanted the girls to look nice. I have never seen anyone half as proud as those children the first day they wore their new uniforms to school.

"Look at them," Agnes said in a rare show of emotion. "It makes all your work on those uniforms worthwhile, doesn't it?"

Once they had their uniforms, our children went to class with new dignity and self-esteem. And later they were even more proud when they won first prize for the nicest uniforms in a competition with other district schools.

About this time it became my responsibility to take care of three babies who had been left with us. This I did in addition to my normal work.

It was during this period also that I was introduced to the ordeal of childbirth, Chinese style. There was no hospital in our village in or any of the settlements within miles of us. We didn't even have a doctor. The problem of assisting mothers-to-be fell to the midwives in the area. I had heard talk about Chinese births but only vaguely knew what went on, so I was completely unprepared for the knock on the door in the middle of the night.

"Miss Kenning, you must come!" one of the servants called to me, excitement shrilling her usually calm voice. "Mrs. Wong is delivering and is in bad trouble. They need you to help hold her!"

I didn't want to go. I was afraid to go; but I was more afraid not to. I had come to China to help the people—that meant a woman in labor as well as a group who wanted to hear about Christ.

The woman who was having the baby was sitting up and a frail Chinese woman was struggling against her convulsive jerking in an effort to hold her still. The midwife was apologetic. She was sorry to have bothered me, she said, but she needed help, desperately. She didn't have anyone strong enough to hold the poor woman.

I took the place of the thin-faced individual behind her, sitting down and grasping the patient with both arms. I suffered with the frightened young woman, experiencing every pain, every contraction. held I her so tightly that my arms throbbed and I had to pray for strength to continue. After the birth, which took hours, life seemed to go out of the mother. She began to hemorrhage and collapsed limply. I was sure she had died in my arms.

The midwife stopped the bleeding before doing anything else. Then she had one of the other women prepare a mixture of vinegar and hot cocoa, which was held under the unconscious woman's nose.

"There's no use," I stammered. "She's dead."

The older woman acted as though she hadn't even heard me. "We have to have the needles! Go get Mr. Suan!"

One of the girls padded silently out into the night, her small feet flying. She returned with the man who practiced acupuncture in our area. He was a somber individual, his face emotionless and his eyes still heavy with sleep. Without a word he went over to the patient, examined her briefly, and removed two long, slender needles from his case. I winced as he pushed them into her taut flesh. He frowned his disapproval of me.

The mother lived and so did the baby, which was somewhat unusual. In our area eight out of ten infants died shortly after birth.

The next time I met a European doctor I asked him about it. The reason was simple. In the West the umbilical cord is cut and tied with sterile surgical thread. In our part of China the cord was cut long enough to tie a knot in it and the end was seared with a hot iron.

"The room where the babies are born is usually next to the stable," the doctor said. "The mat is pushed back and the mother squats on the wood planking in the dust. The opening in the umbilical cord is not properly sealed, so the infant picks up tetanus that comes from the platform. Tetanus is the cause of the majority of infant deaths out here."

After that, whenever I met an expectant mother I stopped and talked to her about the proper way to sever and tie the cord. Infant deaths in our village dropped dramatically.

* * * * *

There were thirty or forty villagers coming to our church every Sunday. Among them was a haggard, emaciated individual who lived in the compound and did odd jobs. None of the Chinese were large, but he was smaller than most. I had been there a year or so when I first heard his story.

He had not always been so gaunt and pinched and poor. Only a few years before he had been one of the wealthiest, most highly respected men in our district, with an elaborate home and servants.

Then he began to smoke opium, the curse of China. It wasn't long until he had lost everything—his family, his home and fields, and all of his servants. He had no interest in anything except his next pipe of opium. Most of the time he was in a lethargic stupor.

That was until he met Agnes and was introduced to Jesus Christ. When he became a Christian he put aside his opium, cleaned up his life, and eventually came to live with us. He was there, puttering around at anything he could find to do, when Agnes' health worsened and she had to return to America.

I don't know whether there was any direct connection between her leaving and his return to his opium or if it was only a coincidence, but not long after Agnes left, he fell back into the habit. The Chinese pastor came to me with the news.

"It can't be!" I exclaimed, refusing to believe it. "He's a Christian. God wouldn't allow a terrible thing like that to happen."

"It's true," he told me sadly. "I have seen with my own eyes."

As soon as he was gone I threw myself, sobbing, onto the bed. One of the people left to my charge had slipped back into sin. I was responsible for him and I had failed!

For two or three days I didn't even want to eat and scarcely moved from the bed. It was one of the most miserable periods I had ever spent in my life. I don't think I would have gone to church on Sunday had it not been for the fact that everyone expected me to be there.

I went in late and took a seat near the front. I had only settled onto the hard bench when someone in the congregation started a song, as was the Chinese custom, and everyone joined in.

"In the cross, in the cross, be my glory ever. . . ."

The Lord preached a sermon to me through that song. "Can you say the cross is your only glory?" He asked me. "Have you been crying and feeling so badly because one of My children has strayed from Me, or do you have another reason? Is it shame because you are afraid people will think that *you* have failed?"

I tried to argue that my only concern was for the Chinese man, but I realized I was not being completely honest. Oh, I was grieved about my friend and fellow worker, but I was also shamed. When Agnes had to leave for America I felt proud of my new position of responsibility—as proud as I was uncertain as to whether I would be able to handle it. Now that one of her most trusted people had fallen into sin, I was afraid of what my fellow Christians might say. They would compare Agnes and me. I imagined I could hear them.

"She's so young and immature, it's no wonder she wasn't able to give him the spiritual guidance he should have had to keep him true to his faith."

"She's just not able to handle so much responsibility."

"We should be praying that God will raise up someone who is older and more experienced."

Those were the things I was more deeply concerned about than our backslidden brother. I was thinking about Grace Kenning and her reputation as a missionary. I wanted people to see what a good job I was doing.

Then God spoke to me again.

"What other people think about you or your ability or judgment means nothing at all," He whispered. "Forget about trying to build a reputation. Forget about impressing other people. I am the One you must deal with. I am the One you must answer to. And I know the intent and purpose of your heart."

That smote me. Had I not been sitting in church with others all around I would have fallen on my face before Him. All that He said was true. I learned a lesson that morning that I have never forgotten. I have often wondered whether God permitted that man to fall away so He could teach me that lesson.

A couple of years later the opium smoker came back to Christ, burned his pipes and turned away from his sin. He remained true to his Savior the rest of his life.

Chapter 7

Pastor Chang—Yes and No

I cannot remember the first time I met Hsing Ting Chang. When Agnes and I moved to our second location, he was already living there. He had been born in that village and had been in business there for a number of years.

I knew he was a widower because he had three children at the orphanage and came by to see them from time to time. I also learned that Agnes had a great deal of respect for him. He was a man of wisdom and ability and great spiritual depth. When the need arose for a new pastor in the church, he was the one she asked to pray with her about it. And when she told him the Lord had been speaking to her about asking *him* to serve the church, he confessed that God had been talking to him about it too.

"Give me a little time to sell my business," he told her, "and I will go into the ministry. I know God is calling."

During that period I was scarcely aware of him as a person. I saw him as I saw the other Chinese Christians, a friend in Christ, but that was all. I can't recall having had even one casual conversation with Pastor Chang during the first two or three years I knew him.

The last admonition from my mother as I was leaving Boston was not to marry a Chinese. "I don't want to have to walk down the street with a couple of slant-eyed grandchildren," she warned me. There was laughter in her voice, but I knew that she meant it.

"Don't worry," I assured her. "I'm not going to be thinking about marrying anyone—at least for a long time. I'm going to China to serve the Lord."

I began to compare Pastor Chang with the young men I had known socially before I came out to China. They were Christians, just as he was, but there the similarities ended. Where they were flippant and flighty, he was serious and stable. Where they were selfish and interested chiefly in good times, and "the better things of life," he was concerned about others and doing the will of God. If that meant having all the material things one could wish for, he thanked God for it. If it meant going hungry or denying himself, he thanked God for that too. He had a singleness of mind that I admired greatly. I always felt that I could do more for God when I was working with Pastor Chang than with anyone else.

When I went to other Chinese believers with a question or for guidance, I was always uncertain as to the motive behind their answers. I was afraid some of them were telling me what they thought I wanted to hear, rather than voicing their true opinions. When I asked a question of Pastor Chang I always got a straight reply. I might not like what he had to say, though he was always kindly, but his words were simple and direct and came from his heart. I learned to value his counsel highly. But I was not aware that I had a personal interest in him.

A year or so after Agnes went home, Pastor Chang had a letter from a pastor friend who lived in another area. I was the only one in the house who was unaware of the contents of this letter, or so it seemed. Our cook informed me of it as she brought in another bowl of rice.

"Isn't it wonderful about Pastor Chang?" she asked.

I looked up, perplexed.

"Haven't you heard? Pastor Chia is going to arrange a marriage for him."

Marriage! Bewilderment gripped my heart. Marriage? It couldn't be! He could never belong to someone else! But what was this feeling I had?

I had never experienced jealousy before and I refused to recognize it for what it was. I tried to make myself believe that I was concerned about the effect marriage would have on his ministry. The people might not like his wife . . . or she might entice him to leave our district to go to her home village. I had a hundred reasons for the way I felt.

Had anyone told me I was jealous I would have been furious! The thought was ridiculous. We had never even gone out together, except to some church activity where we were both taking part.

My fingers loosened on my chopsticks and they clattered noisily into the bowl. I looked away quickly to keep the cook from reading the dismay in my eyes. But I was not fast enough; she saw there was something wrong.

"Are you all right, Miss Kenning?" she asked.

"All right?" I managed a smile. "Of course I'm all right."

"I thought perhaps you had taken sick."

"I'm quite all right. It's just that I—I'm surprised. Somehow I always figured he would remain single."

"We all did." She was chattering excitedly. "We never thought he would permit anyone to arrange another marriage for him."

I ate in silence until she came to bring me more tea. "Do you know who the girl is?" I managed.

"I don't think it's anyone he knows. Pastor Chia sent his picture and a letter telling all about him to the girl's father . . ."

"Then"—I found a certain comfort in the thought—"the arrangements haven't actually been made yet?"

"They've just started," she said, stopping at the doorway. "But what single woman would turn down a man like Pastor Chang?"

I was sick and weak inside.

I don't remember finishing my meal or just what I did afterwards. I knew about the Chinese custom of arranging marriages, of course, but I was not aware of how long the negotiations might take. I had a host of questions, but I didn't want to put any more to the cook. So I sought out one of the other servants and casually asked about it.

The first step was for the father of the young man, or a go-between, to get the reaction of the girl and her family to the proposed alliance. Once that was accomplished, financial arrangements were made. They could take a long time or no time at all, depending on the situation.

There was always a possibility, I decided, that the negotiations would break down—but I could not count on that. No girl in her right mind would pass up an opportunity to marry *him*. I knew what I would do if he did marry and bring his wife to our village. I would leave and go a thousand miles away.

Even with that damning evidence, I still would not acknowledge that my interest in him was personal. He was such a fine person, I told myself, that I did not want to see him hurt or his ministry ruined. I had already decided that the girl Pastor Chia had contacted was not nearly good enough for Pastor Chang and would be a blight on his ministry for the Lord.

That night there was a get-together of some of the believers at a nearby home, Pastor Chang included. As we all sat around, someone mentioned the letter. The openness with which such things were discussed was surprising to me; Americans would have carried on such an activity in the utmost secrecy. Here, they were discussing it as freely as a trip to Tientsin.

I don't know why I did it, but I turned to Pastor Chang during a lull in the conversation and said softly, "When you get an answer to your letter, will you tell me?"

He looked queerly at me as though trying to read my mind. I blushed violently.

"Of course," he murmured, "if you want me to."

The next month dragged by. I didn't dare ask Pastor Chang if he had gotten an answer. Instead I prayed a lot and suffered in silence, wondering with each mail if the letter had come. Finally he appeared at the door with an envelope in his hand.

"It came today," he said quietly.

I stared at him, unable to see how he could be so calm.

"What did she say?" I asked.

"She turned me down," he replied without emotion.

I was amazed at the relief that swept over me.

We did not talk of love, not then. I think he sensed that I was not quite ready for it.

However there was a subtle change in our relationship. I doubt that anyone else noticed at first, but we were spending more time together, enjoying each other's company. It was a year or more before we spoke to each other of love.

We now began to talk openly of marriage, but it could not be before I came back from furlough, I decided. I had to tell my mother face to face about Pastor Chang.

Soon after arriving home on furlough I told her my plans. I hadn't realized the depths of her concern about my marrying an Oriental, but she refused to oppose me.

"Are you sure you love him?" she asked.

"I'm positive."

"Perhaps you will change your mind, now that you are away from him."

I shook my head. "I will always care for him the same way," I answered.

"I can't ask you to go against the dictates of your heart," she said. "You're doing the same as I did when I fell in love with Henry, but I hope you are weighing the cost. A lot of people won't understand."

For me, there was no cost—only the promise of more happiness than I had ever known. I soon learned, however, that mother understood the thinking of our friends much better than I did. Opposition immediately surfaced, bitter and uncompromising. The prospect of marrying a *Chinese* was unthinkable. It would destroy my testimony on both sides of the Pacific, I was told. Neither Pastor Chang nor I would be respected by our people . . . and if we had children they would be social outcasts!

But the more pressure that was applied to stop me marrying the man I loved, the more determined I became to go through with my plans. I bought a wedding dress to take back with me.

A few days before leaving home for my return to China in 1927 I was at a prayer meeting where I was asking the Lord to equip and prepare me for whatever He had in store for me during the coming term. Suddenly, in my mind, I saw a cross on a small hill and my beloved Pastor Chang was at the foot of the cross.

"Are you willing to lay him down?" the Lord asked me. "Are you willing to give him up if I ask you to?"

I could not understand the reason for that. Even today I do not know why it had to be so. All I am sure of is that God wanted me to give him up—whether for a time or for eternity was not clear. But I was not to even think about marriage until the Lord gave me freedom to do so.

Back in China, telling Pastor Chang that I could not marry him—at least for a while and possibly never—was agonizing.

"God would not lead that way," he protested.

"But He has."

"What about our prayers together before you left for home?" he asked. "What about the assurance we both have had that we were in God's perfect will for our lives? He led us together, Grace. He would not separate us now."

I could not explain, but I had to place God first.

"You are free to marry someone else," I told him.

"That will never be. I love you." His lips trembled.

I had to fight to control my tears.

When he saw that it was useless to try to get me to change my mind, he accepted what I had said. "Will you be staying here, Grace?" he asked.

"I don't think I'd better, Hsing Ting."

"Yes, it will be easier if we don't see each other; easier for both of us."

My heart was breaking when we said good-by.

Chapter 8

The New Missionary

Just before I had returned to China, the parents of a girl who was going out for her first term had contacted me.

"Geraldine is about your age," her father told me, "and she's going to China as a missionary, but I'm concerned about her traveling alone."

"I can understand that."

"If you could take her as far as Peking, I'd be grateful. She will be going to language school there. She'd be a companion for you on the trip, and I know you would be a great source of assurance for her."

When I met Geraldine I was surprised to see that she was shorter than I by several inches and as frail as an elm seedling. She looked as if a stiff wind would whisk her away if she didn't expire of fright first. And there was fear in her eyes—a haunting fear of everything around her. While she was talking to me she was continually looking about, her gaze stabbing to my right, to my left, and behind me.

As I got to know her I was troubled about her personality; I should have foreseen the problems that would develop for her in a place like China. However, I recalled my own turmoil when the time had come for Ella and me to sail from home shores. Remembering the people who eight years earlier had helped me to adjust, I pushed aside my doubts about her ability to handle life in a foreign land.

Geraldine asked scores of questions about China before we sailed.

"What is the weather like in your part of China? The winter, I mean."

"It's very much like the weather here in Boston, but it seems colder because they don't heat the houses very well."

"What about colds?"

"People catch colds everywhere," I said, shrugging it off. "If you catch a cold, you get over it in a week or two."

"That's one thing that bothers me," Geraldine replied. "I'm terribly afraid of catching a cold over there. . . . I have weak lungs, you know."

* * * * *

We left America and sailed for China. When we got to Peking I decided to tarry there a while. I had several things to do before going back to my station, and I suppose I was dreading my coming confrontation with Hsing Ting and subconsciously wanted to put it off as long as I could. Geraldine and I shared a room which was more than adequate. I could have been comfortable living in it for my entire term. Geraldine, however, was afraid to stay there.

"I'm getting the sniffles already," she said after her first night in the room. "If I don't get a warmer place I just know that I'm going to catch a cold." Her voice crescendoed . . . "I might even get pneumonia!"

"Would you mind terribly if I moved into the language school building?" she asked. "It would be so much better for my health."

She moved into the three-story foreign-type building, and for a little while she was very happy. But the move did not solve her problem. Before the month was out she had caught pneumonia. She wasn't ill very long, however, and I expected her to go back to her language study. Instead she decided to go with me to the country.

"I can see now that the real work for Christ is being done in the rural areas."

"That's right," I told her. "But the work isn't easy there."

"That doesn't matter," she said, as though she was following the dictates of some divine revelation. "That's where I want to be."

Even at the time I knew I should have refused to take her with me, but my heart was in the villages . . . and I was convinced that God speaks to each of His servants. Rather than question, I accepted her request as being from the Lord.

By this time her instability was becoming more apparent, although I tried to disregard it. I decided that I would help her with the language and get her involved in the work as quickly as possible. She would soon be so busy she would not have time to indulge her preoccupation with herself and her health. I was going to do for her what Agnes had done for me, but without the smothering direction that I had found so chafing.

So when I moved on to another village—after telling Pastor Chang that I could not marry him—Geraldine went with me. She stayed with me the rest of that year and part of the next, learning the language and helping in our work. She did quite well learning Chinese and she could have made an effective missionary, but she was beginning to get restive.

"I miss my piano so much," she complained.

I nodded. There were things from home I missed too.

"I'm very good at the piano, you know. When I was back home I used to practice for two or three hours every day. I'd give anything to be able to do that again."

"Maybe it's just as well that we don't have a piano," I said, trying to tease her out of her black mood. "We've got too much work to do."

Anger clouded her taut young face and her eyes glistened suddenly with tears.

"That's the trouble around here!" she blurted. "You wouldn't understand! . . . Nobody understands!"

Helpless, I watched her run to her room. I had not meant to hurt her and I tried to apologize for what I had said, but she wouldn't come out for the rest of the day.

The morning after her outburst she came to breakfast as though nothing had happened. She was brighter and more cheerful than she had been since we left the city. The following month she was so happy and relaxed I began to think the worst was behind us. Most of the Christians noticed the change in her and rejoiced with me. But then she began to lapse into long, moody silences. She moped about her work, speaking only when it was absolutely necessary, and spent most of her free time in her room. This went on for a week or more until I could stand it no longer. I went to talk with her about it.

"There's nothing wrong," she said icily. "Nothing at all." But in almost the same breath she complained about the lack of cultural advantages in the village where we lived. "I don't see how you stand it out here so far away from everything. You don't have any symphony concerts or organ recitals, or even a choir to sing in. And there certainly is no one around here to talk to who's really stimulating."

I prayed regularly for her, but was not particularly surprised when she announced that she was going to a coastal city to work. "I would like to stay here with you, Grace," she said. "You've been a real friend to me. But I can't stand it any longer; I've got to be where I can advance myself culturally. I've got to be where something is going on."

I looked away, not trusting myself to speak. For an instant or two I was furious. First with her: for being so dissatisfied with the work of the Lord, and for her blind determination to put her own wishes ahead of His leading. Then with myself: for not being able to make her understand the joy that had taken hold of my life since I came out to China, and the peace and satisfaction she could have if only she would serve Him without complaining.

I wanted to shout out my objections and convictions and goad her for turning back from her own commitment to Jesus Christ. But something stayed my tongue.

"When do you plan to leave?" I resignedly asked her.

Her manner quieted as she realized that I was not going to try to persuade her to stay, and for a moment I thought she was about to smile.

"I want the Lord's leading," she said, "so it will take me a little while to decide exactly where I ought to go."

Actually it took her three weeks to find a place of service and somewhere to live in one of the coastal cities. The local pastor and I went with her to the oxcart and said good-by. Tears came to her eyes as we held hands and prayed, asking God's guidance and blessing for her.

"There," I said as the cart rumbled up the dusty road. "She's gone." I did not realize then how stupid that remark must have sounded, but the Chinese pastor was kind enough not to mention it. His heart was going out to the poor, mixed-up young woman.

"She's in great trouble," he said quietly.

* * * * *

I was so busy after Geraldine left that I scarcely thought about her. The Chinese Christians joined me in an evangelistic effort to all the villages in our district. Many of the settlements did not have adequate buildings where we could meet, so I suggested getting a tent.

"That would be fine," one of the men said, "but where can we get anything half as large as we need? Even if we had the money, I don't think there is such a tent in all of China."

"Then we will make one," I announced. There was a certain amount of bravado and ignorance in my words, I must admit, but I really meant what I said.

"You can't be serious," one of the elders countered.

"Why not? In fact, making our own will give us something more practical than if we should buy one. We can design it to fit a threshing floor. That way we'll always have a good, solid place to pitch it."

The men nodded as they understood the advantage that I had just mentioned. The threshing floors in the various villages were all about the same size, laid of heavy timbers to keep the grain off the ground. Pitching the tent on a threshing floor would be ideal.

So we bought material, laid it all out, then sewed it up and attached the ropes, praying about each detail.

Not only did our tent last throughout a full year of hard usage without leaking, but we never once had it blown down.

We would go to a village, get permission to set up the tent on the threshing floor, and start having services. Usually we had three each day. There was one for the children and two for adults. What a glorious time! We never went to a village that we did not have one or two, at least, who became believers. And often there were *many* who made decisions for Christ!

When we left a village we would make arrangements for a knowledgeable Chinese Christian to go back once a week and hold a Bible study for the new believers and those who were interested in learning more about Christ. Those studies often formed the nucleus of a new church.

* * * * *

For several months we had heard nothing of Geraldine, and I supposed the silence was an indication that all was going well with her. Then a visitor from Tientsin came with distressing news.

She had been ecstatically happy when she first moved to the coast. However it wasn't long before she became increasingly unhappy and critical. From there she decided to move to Tientsin. On the train journey there she took ill, began to act queerly, and created a disturbance. She had to be removed and taken forcibly to a hospital. She was being kept in a locked room.

"The doctor wants you to come and talk to him," our visitor

announced, looking at me. "There is no one else who is responsible for her."

The doctor was cold and uncompromising when I talked with him.

"Geraldine has severe mental problems," he said, "and she's apt to hurt someone in her present state. Since she's an alien, she will have to be taken out of the country, immediately."

"B—B—But—" I sputtered. I knew he was expecting me to take her home to the States. I had accompanied her to China. I was an American; so was she.

"I'll give you two weeks to have her out of the country," he ordered. At that, he left me with the problem.

What a problem it was! I had no money for our boat fares. Other missionaries with whom I discussed the situation were sympathetic and promised to pray for us, but none were able to help financially.

I knew Geraldine's parents would have helped if they had known the situation, but there was not enough time to write and get a reply back from them.

In desperation, after much prayer I did the only thing I could think of. "Never be afraid to ask" was a favorite saying of Pastor Chang's. With that in mind, I marched into the nearest bank and asked to borrow the money. I had no account there, I had no security to offer. I simply told them my story—everything.

"It's a bit irregular," the bank officer said, as he fingered his abacus, "but I'll take a chance on you, Miss Kenning. I'll lend you the money."

Geraldine and I were on our way. There were still many long miles and many difficulties ahead for us. I had only borrowed money for our boat fare, but God in His providence arranged circumstances so that we were provided for all along the way.

First there was the long train trip to Shanghai. On a few occasions before we boarded the ship there, Geraldine became difficult to handle and quite violent. However in Shanghai a small prayer group had prayed for her healing. From that moment on she began to improve. There were several minor incidents on the ship that indicated she was still not in full control of herself mentally, but I had very little trouble with her.

When she arrived home practically every symptom of her illness was gone. Her father was completely bewildered and questioned if it had been really necessary to bring her home.

I had to show him the doctor's letter describing Geraldine's condition when he first saw her, and I filled him in on the details of my experiences with her. When he heard that he began to understand.

"We should not have allowed her to go to China," he said when I finished. "It was just too much of a change for her to adapt herself to it."

I nodded in agreement.

Chapter 9

Married At Last

It was five years since God had intervened in my wedding plans and I had said goodby to Hsing Ting Chang. The intervening years had not been easy.

During my first term in China I had never had to do much for myself. When I arrived, my co-worker Agnes was there to do the shopping and make all the decisions. She selected the food we ate and decided when the walls needed painting or the gate needed mending.

Then, after she left, Pastor Chang was there. If we needed onions or rice for the school, I had only to tell him and he would get them in the market at a far better price than I could ever have hoped for. I had only to mention that we needed cloth for new jackets for the girls or that the tile roof needed fixing and he took care of it. I was completely helpless when I first had to look after all of those things myself.

Not only in the practical details of living but also in dealing with people and in matters of spiritual discernment, I had relied heavily on Hsing Ting's judgment.

I had found it difficult to understand why God would not want us to marry at the time we first fell in love. We were both mature adults and engaged in the Lord's work. There seemed to be no spiritual problems to resolve; no human purpose for breaking our engagement. I can only think that God may have been teaching me a lesson in self-discipline to prepare me for difficult days ahead. I certainly had become more independent in the five years I worked alone.

Those years had not been happy ones for Hsing Ting either. His only son, a healthy, intelligent twenty-year-old, contracted tuberculosis and his strong young body wasted away, week by agonizing week. Hsing Ting had taken care of him, himself. For a year he was by his son's side almost constantly before the Lord took him home.

We had seen each other once or twice during those years and had kept in contact with one another. Then sometime during 1933 I seemed to be given the go-ahead to marry Hsing Ting.

So we were married in the summer of 1933 in the province where I was working. I was thirty-three then. I had brought a white wedding dress back to China from America at the end of my first furlough, but when God intervened in our wedding plans, I had used the material for something else. I had to have a new dress and chose a long pink gown.

In the excitement of getting everything ready I completely forgot about ordering flowers. At the last minute we had to go out and pick enough flowers for a wedding bouquet and to decorate the church. They may not have been a fine florist's flowers, but to me they were the most beautiful flowers in the world.

Weddings always played a big part in the village life of our part of China, and our wedding was one of the biggest the province had known. Anyone who had anything to do with the church was there, as well as friends from other places. We were both sorry that Hsing Ting's daughters could not attend the wedding. They now lived far away in another part of China and it was impossible for them to make the trip. In front of our two hundred guests a Chinese pastor friend performed the ceremony and I became Mrs. Grace Chang.

After our wedding I moved to Hsing Ting's station and together we worked for the Lord. We were far happier than I had ever supposed we could be. And with our happiness the effectiveness of our ministry increased also. It was as though God was showing us His blessing by rewarding our efforts with results. Hsing Ting would often smile at me and say, "You have been good for me, Grace."

Then, a week after we celebrated our first wedding anniversary, Hsing Ting took sick. He had occasionally been running a temperature at night. We called in the doctor who pronounced, "Just a sore throat. I'll leave you some medicine. You'd better stay in bed for a while, however."

"How long will it be?" I asked nervously. I was disturbed at having him ill in bed, even if only for a few days.

"He'll be on his feet and working as hard as ever in ten days," the doctor assured me.

"I hope so," I said.

But Hsing Ting seemed to know that there was more to his illness than the doctor indicated. Two or three days later he had me sit by his bed.

"There are some things I have to tell you," he said calmly. "You know that I've bought a piece of land for our family burial, don't you."

I nodded, tears coming to my eyes. Surely it could not be that Hsing Ting had contracted the tuberculosis that took his son. We'd had only one year of happiness together, and now he was giving me instructions for his burial.

In that part of China it was necessary to have a piece of ground large enough to bury the parents and their sons and their wives. Until that was possible, the dead in the family were placed in crypts above the ground. Hsing Ting's parents had had four sons, which meant there had to be space enough for quite a number of graves.

Hsing Ting had bought a piece of ground several years before but had not had his parents buried there yet. His first wife had not been buried either. It was the custom to hold the body of the wife until her husband died and then her body would be interred with his.

"I have ordered my casket," he said quietly and as well composed as though he was talking about a new desk or a chair.

"It has to come from across the river, you know. And if the water is high . . . "

I started to cry. I couldn't help it.

He found my tears disconcerting. "Don't cry," he pleaded, "or I won't be able to tell you any more, and there are some things I should go over with you."

I struggled to dry my tears and allow him to finish. He had arranged for his own funeral in addition to buying his casket, but there was more he felt that he had to go over with me. Chinese customs were so different from those of Westerners that he wanted to explain to me in detail exactly what I should do, for it would all be my responsibility when he was gone.

Were I to do something wrong, the people would probably not interfere—because I was a foreigner. However they would be watching closely to see what I did. Hsing Ting wanted me to be respected and loved by his relatives and the villagers. If I were sensitive to their ways they would respect and honor me for it. My husband knew that, and was determined that I would be able to carry out all their customs in a way that would cause them to respect me.

It was only a few weeks later that Hsing Ting went to be with Christ. After his death, in a last loving act for him, I carried out all his instructions for burying his family. I even ordered a new small casket for the bones of his first wife. Everyone was satisfied with the way I had honored their customs. I know I gained stature in the village.

As for me, it didn't really matter. The happiest thirteen months of my life were over. At that moment I didn't think I would ever be happy again.

Chapter 10

Alone

After Hsing Ting's death I knew I had to get back to work, but I could not return to the village where we had served God together. There were too many memories. I had to go to some place where I was not known, a place where I could lose myself in work. I could not begin to rebuild my life otherwise.

In 1934 I found a village not far from the coast in Chihli (now Hebei) Province, northeast of Peking. Another missionary had worked there for several years, but he had left and no one had taken his place. Shortly after moving there I discovered that there was no doctor within walking distance. Although I had had no medical training, I was often pressed into service to give what help I could.

I will never forget the night I was called to treat my first patient. A very poor family sent one of their sons to get me in the middle of the night.

"My baby sister is very sick," he stammered, his young face white with fear. "My father, he wants that you should come."

"How is she sick?" I asked. My first thought was to get a cart to take her to the nearest doctor.

"Her breathing," he said. "She goes like this . . . " He made the sudden rapid sounds of one with pneumonia or croup who was fighting for breath. "You come?"

"Of course I'll come." I grabbed a half-empty bottle of Vicks the former missionary had left, not knowing if it had retained its strength. When I reached the house the mother already had the straw nearby to wrap the little body in should the baby die. I took a pan of boiling water from the stove, and dropped a generous lump of Vicks into it. I covered both the pan and the baby's head with a large cloth and let her pull the steam into her lungs. It wasn't long until the baby was breathing more easily and had drifted off to sleep. I stayed with her through the night, and in the morning she was much better. After that she recovered rapidly.

My fame with medicine began to grow.

Not long after I had a visitor from another village. A man came in a cart drawn by two horses, an indication that he was quite wealthy. He asked someone about the doctor and was directed to me.

"There's no doctor here," I told him.

"There has to be," he protested. "Everyone has heard about the baby whose life she saved." He insisted that I treat him.

While medicine played a part in my ministry, it was a very small part. I came to the village because a few Christian men wanted the gospel preached there. Those were wonderful days in spite of the grief I was carrying.

I started with children's meetings. There was no problem involved in getting children to come. All I had to do was to let three or four children know where we would be meeting and soon the children would all be there.

In those days it wasn't necessary to have flannelgraphs or hand puppets or even pictures for the children, although that sort of thing would have been nice. I simply gathered them around me, taught them a few simple hymns, and told them Bible stories.

And when we had a meeting for the adults, it was much the same. Everyone would come and listen intently. That isn't to say that they all agreed with the message of Jesus Christ and put their trust in Him. Far from it. But they flocked to hear, an important factor in making the work encouraging.

There were more than nine hundred villages in our province without a single Christian missionary other than myself. It was not possible for me to get to all of them but I visited as many as I could.

It was a fruitful ministry. I have often thanked God that He gave me such a rewarding place to work at that particular time. There were so many children to tell stories to, so many adults to bring the gospel to—and so many decisions for Christ were made that I was busy from early light until long after dark. Had I not had so much to do, it would have been unbearable for me during those months after my husband's death. As it was, one day melted into another. By nighttime I was usually exhausted. So by serving others I was able to bury my personal sorrow.

The village where I made my home saw the greatest results—probably because there was already a nucleus of believers. We had something to build on. We started holding services in a single room with only a few believers, but it wasn't long before a church was built which seated two hundred and fifty. And before we left, a second church seating six hundred was built by the Chinese themselves—and with Chinese money. But that was some years away.

A young pastor had come to serve our growing congregation. Not long afterward, two earnest Christian businessmen came to him with a request. They would like to have a weekly Bible study.

The idea sounded good to the young pastor.

"We'll have to hold it early enough so we can be at our stores by six in the morning," they said. In China the shopkeepers were always in their business places by that hour.

The new pastor wasn't quite so eager about starting so early, but when he saw that the men were set on it, he agreed. To get to the meeting place at five meant that the men who attended had to get up and leave home before their servants were around. They had to draw their own water and take care of themselves. It was probably the only time in years that some of those men had stooped to such menial tasks.

By this time I was spending most of my efforts in the country. Were some of the men from the Bible study to visit a neighboring area and ask the Christians there if they had a weekly Bible study, the people might say, "Oh, yes. We meet every Thursday night."

"That's not what we mean. We're talking about an early morning Bible study," they would reply. That was the genuine article!

In less than a year there were one hundred and fifty attending. And that Bible study became one of the Lord's ways of preserving the church during the years of the Japanese War.

The Japanese occupation force moved into our area in 1935. They had their representatives at every church service, monitoring all that was said, but they sent no one to check the early morning Bible study. There was no question but that they knew about it. However, even after the attack on Pearl Harbor, when they took over the church building and closed down services, they allowed the Bible studies to go on without supervision.

The Communists were active in our area at the same time the Japanese were there. They didn't come preaching their doctrine, but they were in control as effectively as though they had completely conquered the entire province. They appointed the mayors of the villages and the other authorities. They came to us for food and money and, because they were armed, we had to give it to them.

The Japanese were staying along the railroads, except for occasional forays into the countryside, so the Communists had no opposition in the rural areas. They were the only ones who were able to get a true census. How? They didn't go to the family they wanted to find out about. They went next door or to the home of one of their servants.

"How many sons do they have?" they would ask. "How many daughters? Who are the grandparents? Where do they live? How many fields does the father own?"

They found out if the family had a gun and regularly kept ammunition for it. They learned everything about everybody, gathering information for the day when they would take over. We should have been able to read the signs that indicated the Communists were moving to control China, but we didn't. We paid their fees and gave them food and pretended they would go away—if not tomorrow, next week or next month or next year.

* * * * *

I was living in the basement of the new church when the Japanese officer came to arrest me. After being taken to the officer's quarters I spent three terrifying days and nights there wondering about his motives. I prayed constantly, asking God to protect me. He seemed to be waiting for further orders from his superiors.

Finally he had word by radio from his commanding officer. He was to take me back to my home in the church basement and allow me to stay there. How I thanked God for being back in familiar surroundings again. It was wonderful, even though six guards were stationed there to watch me. I remained under house arrest for ten days or so.

One day two truckloads of heavily armed soldiers lurched to a stop in front of the church; machine gunners set up their weapons in the churchyard and bayonet-armed infantrymen jerked open the door and charged inside.

The Chinese villagers saw what was happening and came as close to the church as they dared, crying openly for me. They were sure that I was going to be taken away from them—to a prison or the firing squad. They knew, far better than I did, how cruel their oppressors could be. But God was not ready for them to take me yet. The officer in charge approached me.

"We have investigated you," he said, "and have been unable to find anything against you. You are free to go anywhere in the district that you wish." He paused for a moment. "But you are not to leave the district without written permission from the nearest Japanese Commanding Officer. Do you understand?"

How thankful I was that God gave me such freedom. I had sixteen more months to keep busy there, working for Him. However it was during those months that I took sick. That too was of the Lord, because it taught me two important lessons which later benefited me greatly.

While I was ill God taught me that I had to stop whatever I was doing and rest from nine o'clock to twelve in the morning. I was not to read or crochet or plan the next day's activities. I was to rest.

I had always been one of those individuals who had to be doing something every minute of every day. As I looked at it, an hour of rest was an hour wasted. Now, however, God showed me that I had to take care of my body. I asked Him for the peace to be able to rest in the midst of problems and difficulties. He answered my prayers so wonderfully that I was able to rest even in the most difficult situations. I learned much about rest and peace in those days. It was not the absence of difficulties that made for peace: it was the absence of concern. And only our loving God could give serenity in the face of trouble.

I also learned that it is important for a Christian to be able to say no. Previously, whenever I was asked to do something I had taken it on, sure that it was the Lord's will and that He would somehow give me the strength to do it. The more I worked the more exhausted I became, until my tired body gave up in protest. That was when God revealed to me that He never gives us too much to do. It wasn't long until I reached the place where it did not bother me to turn down a task if I felt that it was too much for me.

I was slowly regaining my strength when a Japanese messenger brought me a note from the commanding officer of the area. "You are to be packed and ready to leave for a concentration camp in the morning," it said.

Stunned, I let the slip of paper fall through my fingers to the floor. It was not for myself that I was concerned, but for the people I was serving. *Who would be there to help them?*

Chapter 11

In Concentration Camp

How word got to our Chinese Christians I will never know, but the soldier who brought me the order had not been gone more than a few minutes when people began to come to say good-by and to tell me that they would be praying for me. A Chinese businessman was the first.

"I'm so glad I was home when this happened," he said. "I want you to take this money."

"I appreciate your wanting to help me," I said, determined that I would not accept it from him, "but I can't take it."

"You must take it."

Then another businessman appeared and likewise attempted to give me money. "You are going to a concentration camp," he said. "You will have to have some money of your own if you're going to be able to get the things you'll need."

"They probably won't let me keep any money if I do have it."

"But they may! You could find that you will have a desperate need for money after you get there, and if you don't take it along now you'll have no way of getting it. You've done so much for us that we want to do something for you."

I was still just as strongly opposed to taking money from them, but I saw how hurt they both would be if I refused. There were several others who personally brought money to me, and that night the church had a special service and took up an offering, so I had a little more.

I was right about not needing money. There was nothing to buy. I tried to keep it with me at first, but when several highly respected prisoners started a bank so the rest of us would not be robbed, I deposited my money with them. When I got home I had forty-five dollars in U.S. funds, all of it given to me by Chinese Christians. I could not help thinking of the goodness of God. When I had reached China in 1919 I had five dollars; when I returned to the States after my internment I had nine times that amount. It was not the money that thrilled me—a missionary soon reaches the place where money doesn't mean all that much. It was the love behind it that made me treasure those few bills.

I packed hurriedly that night after the service. I was permitted to take one trunk. I packed my clothes and bedding, a wash bowl, a slop pail—everything I thought I would need.

I knew enough about the Japanese to know that I should leave behind anything that would attract attention to me. They would be suspicious of every scrap of paper except my American passport, so I left all of those things behind. It was particularly hard to part with my wedding certificate, the last letters I had received from my mother, and my books. I did take along my Bible. At last I was ready to leave.

The next morning they came and took me to the nearest station, where I boarded a train for a larger city in our area. There I spent the night in the priest's home at a large Catholic organization. From there I was taken to a concentration camp at Weihsien, Shantung Province.

We were placed in one long room—men, women and children. I was used to being around Chinese men in all sorts of situations; so having Chinese around would not have bothered me. But seeing white men in the same room was an uncomfortable experience: if I so much as moved my hand I was apt to touch a European or American male. I don't think the situation would have disturbed me had I been like those women who had their families with them, but I was all alone and felt vulnerable and defenceless.

I realize now that they were decent men, trapped by the same circumstances that held me captive, but at the time I felt a sudden anger rise against them. It was almost as though they had contrived to get me into that situation.

I was so miserable I scarcely slept that first night. Exhaustion, bewilderment and shame overwhelmed me. I didn't care whether I lived or died.

There was a lawn chair in the room, and the next day I crawled wearily into it. That is where I was lying when word came that four hundred more Europeans and Americans were being brought in that night.

The information was electrifying.

This new group was arriving from Manchuria after four long days and nights on the train. We all knew from our own experiences that they would be half starved and bone weary. A long train trip in China was a difficult experience at best; an extensive ride under the iron heel of the Japanese army could be traumatic.

"We're going to have to hurry and get ready for them," one of the men declared. "Some of you start pumping water."

It was a relief to be doing something—anything. The men got pails and set to work, drawing water for the prisoners who would be joining us. I was proud of the men and especially of those who so capably took charge. My resentment and anger faded. I was never afraid of any of them again. On the contrary, I thanked God for them.

I have never seen people so close to complete physical collapse as those who got off the train and came stumbling into our camp that night. Their faces were colorless and their eyes dull and glazed from lack of sleep. It was an effort for them to move.

"If you'll line up," one of the self-styled leaders directed, his voice gentle and thick with emotion, "we have water for all of you."

Water! Their lined faces brightened. Water!

"You're the best American in the world!" someone exclaimed gratefully.

The man he was talking to only smiled. He was from England.

Our own weariness was forgotten as we worked, lost in our concern for those whose needs were greater than ours. We labored until two o'clock in the morning in an effort to meet the wants of the newcomers. Seeing their gratitude made us all feel better.

I praised God. For the first time since being ordered to the concentration camp I realized that there was hope. By banding together and sharing each other's burdens, we could survive.

I was not alone in my new sense of determination. Everyone in the camp seemed buoyed up by what had happened. We were no longer a disparate group of individuals, each committed to his own survival: we were welded into a single unit dedicated to the welfare of all. By standing together we would not be broken.

It would have been impossible to collect a more widely differing group of people. We had Catholic nuns and Lutheran and Pentecostal missionaries; criminals straight from their prison cells and college professors; and the presidents of shipping firms and banks. There were no artificial distinctions or social classes among us. Criminal and engineer and preacher worked side by side. Millionaire and the penniless shared a common room. Each was an individual with hurts and needs. Each was as worthy of the concern and help of the group as anyone else.

We had a coterie from Tientsin and Peking to thank for the organization they set up. They had realized that internment was inevitable, and had been meeting secretly to set up a form of camp government which they felt would help us all to survive.

I was afraid that men and women would be housed together in the same room for the duration of our internment, but such was not the case. We were being held in a Presbyterian school compound, and so the single women were placed together, six or seven in a classroom. The students' dormitory rooms were pressed into service for couples.

Although the men from Tientsin and Peking had established our camp organization, we soon voted for the officials we wanted to represent us. One of the missionaries was chosen to be in charge of the work details. The first thing he did was to list the jobs around camp that had to be done on a regular basis. Each person was requested to write down his educational and work background, and to list the three jobs he would prefer in the order of preference. Not everyone got his first choice of tasks, but if he had to settle for second or third choice he sometimes was given a chance later on to switch to something he liked better.

In the early days of our internment the leaders persuaded the Japanese to deal through them rather than directly with each prisoner. They made up the work details, administered camp regulations, and dispensed punishment for infractions. When one brash young girl swore at a Japanese officer, the committee was able to save her from what might have been brutal punishment by administering punishment themselves.

There were over fifteen hundred of us in the compound and our camp government made life a bit easier for all of us, but there were still unbelievable frustrations and irritations. Standing in line in the hot sun was one that bothered me as much as anything else.

We had to stand in line for an hour or two before each meal, and for a similar amount of time afterward in order to wash our dishes. It seemed that we were always standing in line for one reason or another.

It was such little things as taking one's proper place in line that showed the true character of people. Some would never think of stepping in ahead of anyone else. Others did it constantly.

Had I been new to the mission field I would have been quite disillusioned to see the actions of some of my fellow missionaries. Although they were not the only ones by any means, there were a number of missionaries who used one ruse or another to get around the ordeal of standing for an endless amount of time in queues. I was astonished the first time I saw it happen. In the unnatural atmosphere of a concentration camp, such selfishness affected all of us.

There were times when I was tempted to do the same, and times when my temper rose. I found myself having to fight to control myself if, after standing in line for an hour or two, I was told that the kettle was out of food or that they had to change the dishwater. When that happened I wanted to scream at them that it wasn't fair! Why did it have to happen to me? I had to constantly call upon God to put down my ugly, selfish nature and make me sweet and loving in spite of injustices.

The food we were served was an abomination. Our camp government struggled with the problem of providing an equitable distribution of everything while also satisfying the Japanese, who had their own concept of food allotment. Some of our number who had lived in Japan knew that if anything was set aside for later use, then the supply of that item would be curtailed to that same degree.

There were three kitchens, and three large black kettles to be used for cooking. Everything we were given to eat was divided into three equal piles and dumped into the kettles. Everything. Butter, sugar, rice, cabbage, meat or fish—all were thrown in. A yardstick determined the amount of water to be added to each kettle in order to give each of us a cupful of the mixture. The food was almost impossible to eat at first, but we all learned that hunger and passing time will improve even the most uninteresting, strong-smelling stew.

A dietician in the group taught us to skim off the fat and then boil it in cold water to make it clear. This shortening could afterward be added to flour, with sugar, to make something close to a shortbread. Another man was a baker; he took our flour and baked bread for us. So our food improved.

Some people wonder how I am able to enjoy the simple diet I eat today. I tell them I had a six-month training course that has made everything I've tried since taste delicious!

The missionary doctors in our camp deserve credit for keeping most of us well. They had absolute control over our food and watched it closely.

The Japanese food suppliers found a source of overripe fruit. I don't know where they got it, but somehow they brought it in by basketfuls. Some of us objected that it was rotten, but they scoffed.

"It's just overripe," they told us. "You can eat it with sugar or bread, and you'll have something that's both tasty and good for you."

When I finally got home and took a physical I discovered just how excellent our care had been. I had lost only two pounds and was in perfect health.

When it came to listing our preferences for work, my first choice was to be in the kitchen. But I didn't request that type of service because I especially loved to cook—rather, I figured it would be a sure way of meeting some of my friends from Tientsin or Peking who might later be brought to the camp. Sooner or later, those in the kitchen saw everybody.

I felt so alone. I longed for a familiar face. I didn't know a soul in camp when I first got there, but I was acquainted with a lot of people who worked in both major cities in our part of China. Hence my choice.

After I had been in the kitchen a couple of weeks, however, the camp officers decided that the work I was doing was too hard for a woman so I was relieved of my kitchen duties. Shortly afterwards, a missionary friend fell sick; as she was unable to take her five-year-old adopted Chinese daughter to the camp school, I did it for her. I became acquainted with the kindergarten teacher, who soon asked me to help her.

Frankly, I didn't know whether I wanted to help in the school or not. Although the adults were generally self-disciplined and considerate, most of their children were the opposite. Many were the children of highly paid professional and business people. Indulgent "amahs" had done everything for them, and some of them were terrors.

I will never forget my first experience there. The teacher asked me to help a boy who was learning to read. When he got to the bottom of the page, he waited.

"Go on," I said.

He looked up at me, "I will, as soon as you turn the page."

I exploded. "*You* turn the page! And be quick about it!"

He was stunned. Nobody had ever talked to him that way before, but he knew better than to disobey.

I have always loved children, but most of these forty-some five-year-olds the kindergarten teacher and I worked with were completely spoiled. They were rebellious at being made to mind for the first times in their lives. But we were determined that they were going to learn to obey! Eventually we were able to bring a semblance of discipline to our class, but I have always considered that as one of the greatest challenges I ever faced.

Our school may have been short on adequate classrooms, text books and equipment, but our teaching staff was the best. It was made up largely of school superintendents and college professors. Lacking paper, the students doing arithmetic would scratch the answer on the ground with a stick. After the teacher looked it over, the student rubbed out the problem and smoothed the ground for the next one.

I am sure the children gained an education during their time in the camp that could not be surpassed anywhere.

When the time came for graduation, we held a ceremony complete with diplomas. One high school superintendent had brought in a box of blank diplomas when she came. So our seniors were graduated in style.

Every concentration camp has a black market. Ours was operated by a Catholic priest who was determined to help our people. I don't know how he made his contacts, but he was up at two every morning to carry out his clandestine activities. He would hold a long pole over the wall and sympathetic Chinese on the outside would tie to it the items he wanted.

The system he devised for hiding these things from the Japanese was simple, and for a long time it was effective. He would put his contraband in the bottom of a box and cover it with leaves; the garbage men would then put refuse over the leaves, effectively screening the black-marketed items from the watchful eyes of our guards.

He was eventually caught and thrown into solitary confinement. But everyone in camp was so appreciative of what he had done for us that we squirreled away things from our own meager rations and did our best to sneak them to him. Before long, the Japanese released him.

I can't honestly say I thank God that the Japanese placed me in the concentration camp, but I do thank Him for the lessons I learned there.

They have helped me ever since. One of the most important is that the little things of life can make or break you. That is also true of little words.

I remember one time when I was washing clothes. Every drop of water had to be pumped from a deep well, and that was backbreaking work. I had just finished my washing and hung out the sheets when . . . the line broke, and they fell to the ground.

I stared at them. Looking back now, it doesn't seem such a terrible calamity. I suppose it has happened to most women at one time or another. Yet *I was crushed;* that broken clothesline was the end of everything. I felt like leaving them right where they were and running to the end of the world. I don't cry easily, but that morning I felt if I started I would not be able to stop.

Just at that moment someone graciously sensed my frustration. "Never mind," she whispered gently. "You pick up the clothes. I'll pump the water and help you wash them again."

This is the attitude Christ was talking about when He said, "If anyone gives another a cup of cold water in My name, he has done it unto Me."

I had been in Weihsien camp for six months when word came that two hundred and fifty Americans were to be repatriated. I didn't even walk over to look at the list that was posted on one of the buildings until a friend approached, stammering in her excitement.

"You're on the list! You're going home!"

I didn't believe her. "That can't be!"

"See for yourself!"

I went and looked: it was actually true—I was going home. *Home!*

Chapter 12

Home

Our happy group of repatriates was taken to Shanghai by train. What a thrill! Unless you have been imprisoned, you have no idea what the prospect of being free means.

"Look!" I cried, as we passed by St. John's University. "Grass!" I wanted to fall to my knees and kiss it, to take off my shoes and run through it, to lie down and roll over and over in it—to smell that sweet freshness! What anticipation!

One of several girls who had been attending the China International Foreign School felt just as I did. (So that she could go to school, she had been separated from her parents—who were missionaries in unoccupied West China—and she had been caught in the same dragnet that scooped me up.) When finally she was on board ship and it was headed out of the harbor, she ran all over the deck, shouting gleefully (and a bit prematurely), "Now I can write to Mommy and Daddy and the Japs don't have to see it!"

I would have loved to grab that exuberant ten-year-old and hug her. She was doing what we all wanted to do! Yet there was also a weariness about us: the sobering reality that while *we* were headed home, far more of our fellow Americans were still in camps in China and Japan. A large portion of those being repatriated in this exchange were children; so we who were adults could not help asking ourselves, "Why me? What is the reason I am here instead of someone else?" That solemn question kept me awake as I tossed on my bunk at night. "Lord, surely there are many others who are needed at home far more than I."

Then God chided me gently. "Do you question My judgment?" He asked. "I have chosen you to go home now—at this particular time.

You should not feel guilty. I have a job for you at home."

Ours was to be a long trip: with stops at Hong Kong and Manila for more refugees, we spent nearly a month crawling south and west to the Portuguese colony of Goa on the west coast of India. There the Swedish liner *Gripsholm* was awaiting us, and we were transferred from the *Teia Maru* to it. What a change! Now we were finally out of Japanese hands.

The mercy ship *Gripsholm*, clearly identified by giant electrified white crosses on each side, took us southward through the Indian Ocean, around the tip of Africa, and northward through the Atlantic. Because of the danger of being accidentally torpedoed by a German submarine, its deck was brilliantly lit every night and its position at sea was broadcast hourly day and night.

On December 1, 1943, the *Gripsholm* entered New York harbor and was gently pushed into dock by straining tugboats. How we rejoiced to see the Statue of Liberty!

When I reached home I was disturbed to see how much my mother had aged. I had expected her to look the way she had when I left, twenty-four years earlier. Instead, her sweet face was wrinkled and she had great difficulty in getting around. It pained me to see her struggling to get out of a chair.

"She needs me," I realized. "She really needs me."

She had given me to Christian service when I was young. She had prayed for me faithfully all through the years. Now God was honoring her for her devotion to Him: He was giving me back to her in her time of illness.

This was the reason I was part of that early shipload of expatriated Americans. It was for my mother! How I thanked and praised Him.

For two years I lived at home and did deputation, knowing I was in America because Mother needed me but still longing desperately to get back to my people in China. I had great difficulty in adjusting to America and the way the people seemed to be slaves to the clock. In fact, although I lived in the States for over ten years after I was repatriated, I never did get used to the frantic way everyone dashes about. We got things accomplished in China, too, but in a more leisurely way.

Being home with Mother, however, was wonderful, and in spite of myself I began to go back in my mind to those many years when I had been away from her. One afternoon, when the two of us were in the living room alone, she seemed to sense what I had been thinking.

"There's something I want you to know, Grace," she said, suddenly. "The Lord took better care of me all those years you were away than you could have done for me if you had stayed at home."

Again God had shown me I was in the center of His will.

After two years devoted largely to deputation, I saw an ad offering employment for a housekeeper. With Mother's agreement I took this opportunity for work as I would still be able to take care of her. In fact, for the next six years I was able to work, mainly at jobs involving home nursing care. Here I was able to find people in need—people who needed loving care and the love of God.

One person I will never forget was Evelyn Norton, a little girl with a malformed hip, club feet and other serious physical difficulties. For several years I worked with her, encouraging both her and her parents to realize that she could live a full and happy life.

What a day it was when she first learned to walk! Eventually Evelyn grew up and was able to drive a car and take care of herself. I learned later that one of her brothers had become a Christian "because of the nurse my parents hired to look after my sister."

Chapter 13

The Word of God
Will Not Be Destroyed

Mother lived for several years after the doctor discovered that she had cancer. Death was a blessed release for her after months of suffering, and I could not wish her back, much as I missed her. She was with her Lord, which was far better.

After her death I became restless once more. My life had had such meaning during my years in China, but now it seemed to have no direction—no purpose. I had nothing to keep me in America, I realized, and the Lord has such need of people to take the good news of His salvation to those who have never heard. But China was closed, for the Communists had taken control in 1949, and at fifty-two I was too old to learn another language and adjust to a different culture.

Or so I thought.

Restless and confused, I went to a Sunday School conference. On the way home I stopped in a small town near Lancaster, Pennsylvania, to visit a Miss Mary Leaman who had also been a missionary in China. Miss Leaman too had been in a Japanese concentration camp, though a different one than I had been in. I had never met her, but I knew her by reputation. There was something I particularly wanted to thank her for. . . .

* * * * *

Many missionaries and indeed many of the less educated Chinese have difficulty in reading and writing Mandarin. Some thousands of characters have to be mastered. Many of my village Christians could not read at all—certainly they couldn't read the Bible.

Miss Leaman had taken the government's National Phonetic System—a Chinese phonetic "alphabet" of thirty-seven symbols, which, in sets of three, could easily be combined into words—and had written out the Bible in it. It had the simpler phonetic symbols alongside the regular idiographic characters.

A missionary friend had sent me a copy of this system, and after much initial discouragement from some of the better educated Chinese who looked on it contemptuously, I had successfully used it to teach some of our illiterate Christians to read.

I was most proud of a middle-aged beggar woman who had never had a chance in her life. She was somewhat retarded mentally, and had a most difficult time in eking out an existence. But when she received Christ she was determined to learn to read.

We had to go over her lessons again and again. Sometimes it took her four or five days to master a single phonetic symbol. However, she kept plugging along until she finally was able to stand up in church and read from the Bible. The words came out haltingly, but she was able to read. That was the proudest moment of her life and one of the proudest of mine. I will never forget the look of triumph on her face as she closed the Bible with trembling fingers and marched off the platform.

Many of our Christians learned to read with the phonetic symbols, but there was a more important benefit—as they pored over the Bible their faith soared! I had known for years how the Bible could change lives, but I had never seen it more dramatically demonstrated than in my little village in China.

This was why I wanted to meet Mary Leaman and to thank her for her work.

After we talked, Miss Leaman said she had something to show me in the basement. There, in a trunk which she had brought back with her from concentration camp, was a whole set of the original wooden type of the phonetic Bible. When the phonetic Bible had been published in China, metal type was cast from these original hand-carved symbols. I thought of China and the fact that it was now closed to missionaries. Were any of those phonetic Bibles still in use, or had they all been confiscated?

"What a tragedy," I murmured. "All that work lost."

"But it's not," Miss Leaman said. Then, taking me up to the attic, she showed me a set of original proof sheets of the Bible.

"I have another set in a bank vault."

This was truly a miracle that the work had been preserved. It meant that the Bible could be put back into print again.

Miss Leaman had approached the American Bible Society, but had met with nothing but discouragement. The cost of such a project would be too high, they said, and they could find little enthusiasm for it among educated Chinese in the States.

I felt that something had to be done and promised to follow up the matter for her when I returned home.

I too tried the American Bible Society and then the Pocket Testament League, but neither were interested in publishing the Chinese Phonetic Bible.

Someone at the Pocket Testament League told me, "Ken Adams at CLC is the man you want to see. If there's anyone who will catch the vision of something like this and see it through, it is Adams."

I had been acquainted with the Christian Literature Crusade and Ken Adams for some time, but had never thought about them as a vehicle for getting the phonetic Chinese Bible republished.

Now that I realized that this was a possibility, I went by train to Philadelphia and then to the Christian Literature Crusade headquarters in Fort Washington.

They were sympathetic to the project and eager to have a part in getting the Chinese Phonetic Bible back into print. But there was one problem.

"We don't have the money to bring out *all* of it," Adams told me. "Not now, at least. But we could start with the Gospel of John, and as the funds come in we could go from there."

I don't know why I went back to the American Bible Society. They had already turned down the project twice. On this visit, however, God was working. I got to see Dr. Norris himself, and he gave me enough time to present the project. He seemed interested almost immediately.

"We would have liked to have had a chance to do it," he told me. By this time he had come around from behind his desk and was sitting casually on the edge of it.

"We've already given you a chance," I informed him. "I came and talked with some of your people, but was turned down flat. So, we've made arrangements to have CLC bring out the Gospel of John."

"Is it on the press yet?"

"No, but it's going to be there any day now. They have all the copy and are working on it now."

"Will you print three thousand copies for us?" he asked.

I was astounded. We were printing only one thousand copies. The interest of the Bible Society was an indication that God's hand was on our efforts and that He was going to see the project through.

As soon as I got home I called Ken Adams and told him to increase the print order to four thousand copies. Then I called Miss Leaman to give her the good news. That night she called me back.

"I've just had a telegram from the American Bible Society," she said. "The printer in Hong Kong—you know, the one I contacted months ago—got in touch with the Bible Society. His price was so favorable they decided to take on the entire project."

You can imagine what a time of prayer and thanksgiving we had. The next day I was on the train for New York City, where I handed the proof sheets for the entire Bible to the American Bible Society.

Chapter 14

Willing Hands

Several months later, while on a visit to Philadelphia, I went to one of a special series of meetings. To my surprise Ken Adams was bringing the message!

I have always felt that nothing happens by chance for one who trusts in Christ, and even before he spoke I felt that perhaps his message, entitled "Willing Hands," was intended for me. I was deeply touched by what he said and went to his wife after the service. "I want to offer my willing hands," I told her.

She eyed me quietly. "Are those hands willing for a special job," she asked, "or are they willing for *anything*?"

"I've already served the Lord for thirty-four years," I replied. "They're willing for anything."

A few weeks later they were to be having a conference—a combined conference of the Christian Literature Crusade and its sister mission the Worldwide Evangelization Crusade (WEC)—and I volunteered to help Mrs. Adams. She asked me to take charge of the kitchen.

"We don't have the money to underwrite the cost of the meals," she said. "You will have to do your own buying . . . and trust the Lord to bring in the money to pay the bills."

When I volunteered to help, the last place I expected to be was in a kitchen! However, I did not hesitate before agreeing. I had told them I was willing to do anything. That was exactly what I meant.

The conference was considerably larger than we had expected. They had told me to expect as many as two hundred, and we had three hundred in attendance. One of the staff came to me, deeply concerned. "What are we going to do?" she asked.

"We'll have to feed them, of course."

"But it will cost so much."

"I have a theory," I said. "If we give them good food they will pay for it." I set to work preparing menus. We were going to have meat for every meal. Some of the staff tried to cut down on the size of the servings in order to save money, but I put a stop to that.

"These people are hungry," I said. "Let them come back for seconds."

The workers' eyes widened. "Seconds?" they echoed. "Of meat?"

"That's right. I bought half a steer, so there'll be plenty of meat."

They did as they were told—but disapproval was written in their eyes, and I knew there was plenty of talk when I was out of hearing about the extravagant Grace Chang.

It was easy to see why they were concerned. CLC and WEC are missionary organizations, and they were not charging for meals during the conference. People were free to put what they wanted to in the offering boxes. I was impressed to see how they handled the financial arrangements at their conferences. I hadn't expected anyone in America to arrange things this way. It seemed out of character for practical, materialistic America. I was impressed by the way they trusted the Lord for money to take care of the bills. And when I tallied our funds after paying all the grocery bills, we had $1,500 left over!

After that first large conference I was given the responsibility of the kitchen for several smaller meetings. I always tell people that I wasn't a candidate like the other CLC missionaries. "I came in through the back door—the kitchen."

During one of the shorter series of meetings when I was working in the kitchen, I received a letter from Indonesia. Even today I don't recall who it was from or what it said. I only remember that my heart began to burn as I read it. The Lord was speaking to me in a very real way. "This is for you," He was saying.

When I went back into the kitchen after reading the letter I said to the girls who were working there, "I finally know where I'm going."

"Where is it?" they asked.

"I can't tell you," I replied. I would have felt foolish telling them I felt that the Lord wanted me to serve Him in Indonesia with the Christian Literature Crusade. I was almost fifty-three years old, and I had never been out under a board. I had heard that some missions insisted on having youthful candidates. The CLC might refuse to accept anyone as old as I.

Yet I knew that God was speaking to me. I was as sure of that as I had been when He had called me to China as a girl.

As soon as I could, I went to Mr. Adams. He is one of those people whom it is easy to confide in. I shared my concern for missionary literature, reminding him of my experience with the Chinese Phonetic Bible which had made me see the importance of using reading material to reach the hearts of the lost for Christ and in bringing new believers into a closer walk with Him. I told him of my strong inner feeling that God was calling me to Indonesia.

"We don't have any regulations regarding the age of our candidates," he said, "although we prefer younger missionaries. They have a longer time of service after learning the language."

"But there are many Chinese in Indonesia," I said, "and I already speak Mandarin."

"I'm not saying we won't accept you, Grace," he countered quickly. "I was just telling you that we prefer younger candidates."

He gave me an application form to fill out.

The CLC staff had the same philosophy that I did. They trusted in the Lord's leading, rather than the reasoning of men. We discussed my going out to Indonesia, prayed about it, and let the Lord direct my steps. It was decided that I would accompany Willard Stone, a new CLC missionary who was also going to Indonesia. He was from North Carolina, a young man of thirty-five. He had been chosen to open a bookstore in Indonesia.

Everyone anticipated that I would have a long, difficult time getting my Indonesian visa. Most missionaries had to wait for at least two years. But God knew how anxious I was to start serving Him in Indonesia. He opened doors for me . . . and in a matter of weeks I had my visa. This was in July 1954.

Someone in the CLC British headquarters published an account that said Willard Stone and Grace Chang, an elderly Chinese lady, were going to Indonesia. The elderly part was what bothered me! It made me sound as though I was ready for a wheelchair and a retirement home. However, I took no offense at being thought Chinese. There were times when I felt more Chinese than Caucasian.

I was excited about the possibility of helping open up the CLC work in Indonesia. The time was right for a literature ministry in the islands. After the people gained their independance from Holland at the end of World War II, English replaced Dutch as the official business language. The requirement that all education must be in Dutch was also dropped. At that time there were few books in any of the Indonesian languages and dialects, and fewer Christian books, but there was a wide range of English and Chinese material. Fortunately for me, there were many Chinese living there.

We went to Kediri first, a small place in the province of East Java, where the Worldwide Evangelization Crusade had opened a small literature work. It was our responsibility to take it over and expand it.

From the beginning I loved Indonesia. I had never seen so many different shades of green. As we rode along we saw the green of the rice fields . . . and above that the softer green of the banana trees . . . and rimming the horizon, the forested hills.

I found Indonesia delightful and I was happier than I had been since my internment by the Japanese. Because of my Chinese name, my understanding of their culture and my grasp of the language, I was welcomed by the large Chinese community. It was almost as though I was one of their own. There were a large number of evangelicals among the Chinese. They became the base for my ministry with their unconverted countrymen.

On the average the Chinese were more prosperous and better educated than their Indonesian neighbors. And, since many of them were in business, the new emphasis on English made it necessary for them to learn that language. I realized this shortly after we reached our destination and set to work in our bookstore.

"I think we should stock English books," I told Willard.

"The Indonesians won't be able to read them," he reminded me.

"The Chinese will. And because they are so anxious to learn English they are going to be eager to buy English books. I think we ought to take advantage of that."

We began stocking books in English and Chinese in addition to the few titles we could get in the Indonesian languages.

If we had been limited to the books available in Indonesian and had not sold a large number of books in both Chinese and English, it would have been almost impossible for us to have gotten our struggling little bookstore off the ground.

Chapter 15

Books, Books, Books

In Kediri we had our stock of books in the small room just in front of my bedroom. We were not only selling from that location, we were busy sending out parcels of material all over Indonesia. From the beginning we sensed the lack of good reading material in Indonesian. Most of the Bibles, for example, were printed and bound in Holland. But when the Dutch residents were finally forced out of the country in 1957, the source of Indonesian Bibles was gone, and it was a number of years before other publishers took over.

Because of my love for the Chinese in the community I felt a real responsibility for seeing that they had all the Christian literature they could use. Yet I was upset about the situation that faced the Indonesian pastors and Christian workers. They would come in and look longingly at the books in full color that were available in Chinese and English.

"And you don't have *anything* for us that looks like this?" they would ask, fingering one of the beautiful new books for children.

"I'm sorry," I said, "but there is nothing available."

They would look up at me, questioning. "Why?"

I had no answer for them, but that look kept me from sleeping at night. "I won't be satisfied," I told the Lord in the quiet of my room, "until we have beautiful, good quality books in Indonesian."

Willard Stone shared my concern for literature in the language of the people, and we put it at the top of our prayer list.

God soon made it possible for us to move in that direction. With the help of Moody Press we were soon able to obtain *Bible Pictures for Little Eyes* by Kenneth Taylor. We had two editions printed in America and sent out to us in unbound sheets. The art work was printed from the plates of the American edition but the English words were omitted. We printed the text in Indonesian and had the books bound locally.

"Isn't it wonderful, Grace?" Willard said as we saw the interest in the new book. "God is beginning to give us the kind of literature the people want."

* * * * *

Willard and I had not been working long in the small city of Kediri before it became evident that we would have to move if our ministry was to grow.

"We've got to get to a large center of population, Willard," I told my fellow missionary.

He looked up from what he was doing, deliberately.

"We've got to be in a place where we can attract more customers," I continued. "That's one thing. And we're concerned about getting books brought out in Indonesian. In a place like this we can't get translators and printers, but in a bigger city we would have both."

He nodded. "I've been thinking the same thing," he drawled. "It seems to me that Surabaya is the place we ought to move to—if we can find a suitable location."

"When do you think we can go in to see about a location?" I asked. I'm quick and impulsive by nature. I want to see things *move*. If I feel the Lord wants a certain activity undertaken, I'd like to have it done yesterday!

Willard wasn't so sure when he could get away. There were shelves to stock and orders to fill. "Besides, we want to be sure that we are making the right move. We've got to be sure that we choose the right location."

I turned and went back to my books, trying to work off my frustration. If I had had my way we would have been packing to move, but Willard had to ponder over it—considering every aspect of the entire situation before making a move. At last we left Kediri for Surabaya, the largest city in East Java, and began to look for a suitable building.

Suitable property for retail businesses was scarce in the city. When we did find something that looked as though it had possibilities, Willard had to go over it painstakingly as though he was going to buy it. Methodically, he went into every detail of the construction of every place we considered. He had to examine the roof for leaks, plus the doors and windows, the plumbing and wiring.

"We're not going to *buy* the place, Willard," I would remind him with less serenity and composure than I should have had. "We just want to rent for a bookstore."

"I know," he answered quietly, "but these things are important. It is never wise to make a decision quickly. The Lord wants us to be careful."

I think that was the part that bothered me the most during the years we worked together. I am geared for action, not caution. I would whip into an empty building, take a quick look around, and decide in twenty minutes whether I liked it or not. If I didn't—and that was usually the case during the long period of searching—I had another address in my handbag, and would soon be off in another pedicab to look elsewhere.

I used to groan inwardly at my fellow missionary's indecision. "Willard," I would say to myself, "can't you *ever* make up your mind?" There were times when I was short with him and God would convict me of it. On those occasions I would go to him.

"I'm sorry, Willard," I would say contritely. "I shouldn't have spoken to you the way I did."

"That's all right, Grace," he would answer. "Don't think anything more about it. I'm not going to." I had the impression that he knew my temperament and scarcely even heard me when I was curt and unkind to him. That same cautious, easygoing way that I found so difficult to understand helped him to be infinitely patient and forgiving.

Looking back, I can see that God placed us together because of the differences in our temperaments. I was a goad to Willard, constantly trying to prod him into action, so we could move on in the job God had called us to Indonesia to do. He was a brake to my impetuous ways.

Nevertheless, Willard tramped the streets tirelessly, running down every lead, looking for a place that was suitable. There were a number of shop buildings available, but closer examination would show us that the location was all wrong, or there was some other problem that made the place undesirable. But as we combed the city, our standards for a building went down and down. We hit the point where we were considering any place that would give us a bit of room to display our books.

Though we were selling a certain amount of reading material to the Christian Chinese we came in contact with, we weren't reaching many who didn't already know Christ as their Savior. This disturbed us both. We had come out to Indonesia with the goal of presenting Christ to the *lost* through the printed page. Yet there seemed to be nothing we could do to make that possible.

Finally we found a place—the best we had been able to discover. But it was on a back street, on a narrow, twisting lane. We told the woman who owned it that we would take it, yet both Willard and I were heartsick.

"It just isn't suitable at all," he said.

For once I agreed completely with him. It was one of those times that comes in the life of everyone, including missionaries, when it seems that even God has forgotten us.

But He had not.

God had been waiting for us to reach the end of our own ingenuity. We had exhausted every lead. Now, after two months of futilely combing Surabaya, we were sure there was not one location that would be satisfactory for a bookstore.

But then I went to the Chinese church in the city, and a woman came up to me and insisted that I go home with her for supper. I thought it strange at the time, since I hardly knew her. However, a young Christian Chinese businessman who had been one of our book customers in Kediri was there.

"How is your bookstore going?" he asked.

"We have felt led to move it to Surabaya," I said. "It's been most difficult trying to find a place for it; however, I think we have one now." I then told him about the house we had rented and that we planned to make the front room our bookstore.

He knew the location, and disappointment clouded his face. "That's in a residential area," he said. "It isn't even near a business district. You're not going to get much trade from off the street."

"It's the best we could do," I told him, a bit short.

"But people aren't going to be able to find it," he went on.

I was irritated at his persistence but I tried not to show it. "We've been searching for the past two months," I told him, "and it's the best we've been able to find."

"I've got a little shop building you can have for your bookstore . . . if you want it," he said casually as though he was asking me to have a cup of tea. "However, you would have to find a separate place to live, Mrs. Chang," he continued, "for there isn't enough space for living quarters too. But the location is good. With the numbers of people who are on the streets in that area you ought to do very well. . . . "

I was so stunned I didn't ask him any questions about it. I didn't know where it was or how large it was or how much rent he wanted. I mumbled something or other to him . . . and went back to the house where I had a room. I told the people there what had happened. They got more excited than I.

"Grab it quick, Grace," they said. "We've been praying about that building for the last two weeks. We knew it would make an ideal place for the bookstore, but we didn't dare to ask him about it."

I contacted Willard as quickly as possible. For once he moved quickly. We both decided that I should see the young Chinese businessman as soon as possible and find out what it would cost us to rent the place. I went over to see him at seven o'clock in the morning. Willard would have been more considerate and waited until eight or nine, but I had to get to the house and see the man as quickly as I could.

He had just finished his bath and was still in his wrapper when I knocked on his door. I'm sure he wondered why I had shown up at such an hour, but he was too kind to ask. He invited me in and I sat down across from him.

"This is business," I began abruptly. "What did you mean when you said we could have your building for our bookshop?"

"Just what I said," he explained. "You can use it if you want to. As soon as I get dressed we can go and look at it, if you want to."

I hesitated. Did I want to look at it! Actually I wanted to do more than that. I wanted to lease it on the spot before he could change his mind.

"H—How much does it lease for?" I stammered.

He seemed surprised. "I thought I told you. You can *have* it if you want it."

"Y—You don't mean that it would be rent free, do you?" I blurted.

He nodded. "That's what I had in mind."

The location was even more ideal than we could have possibly hoped for. It was in the Chinese district at the end of the bus line, and the post office was less than two blocks away. We did a great deal of mail-order business, which meant that we had to make a lot of trips to mail packages, so this was important. We were overjoyed at the way God had answered our prayers.

The other building we had been considering we decided to rent as living accommodation for me, and it proved to be an ideal place in which to live.

In our new location the bookstore prospered. It wasn't long until it became self-supporting. At least we were able to pay our bills and order the new stock we needed. Of course, we had two important advantages: for the first twelve years we did not have to pay any rent; and those of us who worked at the bookstore did not receive wages from it. Still, we felt the accomplishment was encouraging.

During the early days of our operation in Surabaya we saw the struggling new nation of Indonesia rocking uncertainly on its financial legs. Inexperience, corruption and political rivalries joined forces, causing inflation to spiral. The value of the rupiah dropped to practically nothing in comparison to the dollar and every other stable currency.

One morning a radio announcement advised us of a drastic change in the value of the rupiah. The five hundred rupiah note became fifty rupiahs and the one thousand rupiah bill became one hundred. In essence 90 percent of our money was taken away by the stroke of a pen. A little later they required everyone to turn in his old bills for new. A charge of 10 percent was made for the transaction, which further decreased the amount of money in the hands of the people.

The richer families—and especially the Chinese—kept their money in goods, so they were not affected very much. It was different with the poor. They became still poorer and suffered a great deal. I remember crying as I walked down the streets and saw the bloated stomachs of the children and the sunken eyes and vacant stares of their parents. There was little anyone could do to alleviate the suffering. Until the new rice crop was harvested the people had little to eat except cassava root, which provided nothing but carbohydrates.

It was difficult running a bookstore in those days, and I am still not sure how we were able to survive—except that the Lord kept His hand upon us.

We had help from unexpected sources. During an eight-year period beginning in 1952, a campaign to stamp out illiteracy was underway. Several million people learned to read, and they had an almost insatiable desire for books. Our books were reasonably priced, and our colporteurs, fanning out into the villages, were able to sell hundreds of copies at each stop. I will never forget the time two young missionaries, John Capron and Jeff Gulleson, sold 385 books in a single hour.

"It was great!" John told me when they got back to Surabaya. "We were so busy we hardly counted the money. Just stuffed it into our pockets and hoped that we had collected the right amount."

I don't remember who had the idea of bringing out a calendar with colored pictures. There are many different kinds available now, but when we first came out with ours it was *one of a kind.* I have never seen people so excited about anything. The day we put them on sale things almost degenerated into a riot as men and women pushed and shoved into the packed store to get a copy before we ran out.

"Willard!" I cried, "We've got to get them out of here before they wreck everything!"

Somehow we pushed them out onto the street and locked the door. Gradually the crowd retreated and order was restored. After that we admitted only a few people at a time until the calendars were gone.

That was the first of our yearly calendars. Missionaries have told me of going into a humble hut far in the interior and seeing one of our calendars five or ten years old on the wall—still cherished!

I had the opportunity in Surabaya to get acquainted with many very poor people. There used to be a stand near our store where pedicabs congregated, waiting for fares. The store had windows at the front that angled back to the door, and some of the drivers would close off the little area at night and sleep there. I got to know them well, and there were two or three who seemed to enjoy taking me places. Willard and the other missionaries accused me of having them "on the payroll," they were so anxious to serve me.

One morning a stranger came into the store, snatched up the adding machine and ran out with it. One of my special driver friends saw it, jumped on his pedicab, chased the thief and caught him. Triumphantly he came back with the machine.

"That's very unusual," one of the veteran missionaries said. "Most Indonesians think that all foreigners are wealthy, so they would have done nothing about getting the adding machine back." He turned to me. "You must have a very special place in the hearts of these pedicab drivers."

Chapter 16

New Horizons

After a furlough in 1961 I arrived back in Indonesia for my second term. I tried to keep my co-workers and prayer partners in the U.S. regularly informed of our activities. Here are excerpts from several of my letters.

May 10, 1962

Dear Ones at Fort Washington:

We do appreciate your prayers for us here. Just one instance to show you how the literature work is absolutely dependent on prayer. Willard put in an order with Japan Sunday School Association last year for picture blanks, to be delivered in September 1961. He was counting on having the book texts printed here and ready for last Christmas.

Well, one printer, being busy, let the work out to another, and in the end the goods arrived in Tokyo with the colors mixed up. Some pictures were printed in the wrong places, some were upside down, etc. The entire order was unsalable and needed reprinting. We hope they will be shipped this month. So nothing can be counted on in the natural—each project needs continued prayer until the books are in the hands of the people.

In July there is to be another Chinese young people's conference with over five hundred gathering from all over Java, and from outside. We are preparing for that, and have sent quite large orders to Hong Kong. When I arrived there, one publisher greeted me with the news that he had ninety-six packages of books packed and ready for Indonesia.

I arrived back here and found everyone well and busy, praying for wisdom for the next advance. In many ways they like the new store much better than the old one. It is more roomy, though not quite as large. However the door is wide open all day and the dust just rolls in from the street. When I saw the beautiful new store in Bangkok I had to pray and ask the Lord that I might not be jealous.

For the present I am settling in to my two rooms. Must confess that my heart sank as I entered the closed-up, dark, musty-smelling place. While Willard was in Palembang there was a flood on this street. Twelve inches of water flooded the rooms. Imagine the mess of trunks, books, etc.

He had the whole mess cleaned up, the things in my trunk washed, etc., but still the musty smell was about all I could take. Quite a welcome back from the States! Such is life on the field. It has its joys and sorrows. There is a lesson in all of this. We should hold onto the things of this world very loosely.

Greetings to all,
Grace

* * * * *

June 24, 1962

Dear Ken and all at headquarters:

Just this past week we have had a wonderful answer to prayer. We prayed for wider distribution of literature. The Lord sent along a Catholic priest from another island who wanted to buy twenty copies of *The Bible in Pictures for Little Eyes* in Indonesian. Our first reaction was to limit him to ten copies. Then I felt an inner check. I said to my fellow worker who was waiting on him, "Let him have them and pray that they will bring a message of life to those into whose hands they come." Our problem is that we only have two thousand copies. We must be very careful about how we distribute them.

A few days ago I said to Willard, "The time is short. I feel that we should go ahead in faith and order at least five thousand of the picture blanks for *The Lost Sheep*." He agreed, and I was to send off a letter inquiring what others were going to do. That letter had not even been sent before your letter announcing the gift was received. It was enough to cover three-fourths of the cost of printing twenty thousand copies. So, there was no question in anyone's mind but that we must go ahead, trusting the Lord to complete what He has begun in such a wonderful way in His way and in His time.

You need to continue to pray, "Bibles for Indonesia, Lord." Now add to that request, "Chinese Bibles for Indonesia, Lord." I came back to find that there was not a single Chinese Bible to be bought anywhere in Indonesia.

Pray for the conference of over five hundred Chinese young people at Malang Bible College, July 4–8. Many of those who are now in Bible College dedicated their lives to the Lord in just such a conference.

Pray for the health of all workers. Pray for much wisdom for every angle of the work. Many times we do not know what to do from day to day.

Counting on your prayers.

Grace

* * * * *

September 26, 1962

Dear Bess:

Your good letter has just come to hand, and as I am in the mood I will do something that I very, very seldom do—and that is, write a letter in the store. Your letter made me almost homesick to be with you all again.

I have some important news that I must share with someone. (I have been sworn to secrecy here.) Willard has just told me about his intention to get married to Dottie Brooks. I was really surprised, but am a hundred percent for it. I think it would make a great difference in him, and will also be very good and even necessary for the future of our work here. I cannot understand why he did not say something sooner. I don't think there should be any trouble in her getting a visa to come back into Indonesia with him. They call it a "following-the-husband visa."

In all, it will mean six to nine months out of the country for him. I hope you at home sanction Willard's getting married.

All my love,

Grace

* * * * *

June 24, 1963

Dear Praying Friends:

Once again I can tell you that the God of the Impossible has again heard and answered your prayers. Shortly after sending the requests for prayer, I could feel the burden being lifted. The problems were still there, but I was on top of them. As my mother used to say, I could ride the camel.

Within two weeks after applying for her visa, Willard's wife had it. They even surprised me by walking into my yard two days before they said they would arrive. I was shocked, but very happy—though none of the preparations we hoped to have completed were done. Still, the Stones were so happy to be here at last that they took me as I am.

That was June the fifth. On the tenth we had a small reception for them with about eighty guests attending. They had only been married for a month.

Dorothy has been coming to the store each day. I am so thankful that the Lord has sent us one who is already trained in Christian literature work. (Dorothy has worked in a Christian bookstore in the States for eight years.) It does make a difference when one does not have to tell a new worker every little detail.

This week Dorothy will have to start her most important task for the present, that of learning the Indonesian language. She will have to study for the major part of each day. While she will not come to the store regularly now, we can look forward to the time when she will. Please pray for her as she studies. We have already found someone to teach her.

The lost typewriter has not yet been found, but I am learning lessons through the experience. The Lord supplied a very bright and quick young Chinese man to help us for a few weeks. The Lord answered prayer and undertook for us, so the burden was not too heavy.

Greetings to everyone,
Grace

* * * * *

March 9, 1964

Dear Praying Friends:

I have had to lean heavily on God's promise, *"As thy days, so shall thy strength be.*" I have found it to be true. I have not missed a day at the store, except for my recent two weeks in the hospital. Here is what brought that about.

One afternoon I was on a busy corner in downtown Surabaya when a truck turned in front of me and ran over my feet with the rear wheels. Bones in both feet were broken and I was taken to the hospital. My feet are in casts that extend six inches up my lower legs. Right now I am sitting here in Willard's home, as blind as a mole—for when the truck ran over my feet and knocked me down, my glasses were broken. They are now being repaired.

I had three women who shared my hospital room with me.

"Have you any children?" one of them asked me. "And do you have any family here in Indonesia?"

"No," I said. "I have no children and I have no family here."

They were genuinely concerned for me. "Oh, that's too bad," they said. "You must be very lonely."

Then so sweetly the promise of the Lord came to me, and I changed my answer. "Oh, but I have a hundred children."

They both thought that was a big joke and laughed with me. But in the next few days the Lord proved Himself in the fulfillment of His promise to give everything in this life to those who have left father, mother, sister or brother for His sake.

On the day of the accident I had just come back from the x-ray room and hadn't even been put to bed when a businessman came to the hospital to see me and find out how badly I had been hurt. Willard had also heard about it and came from the store, arriving almost at the same time as the other man.

That was just the beginning. Every day, twice a day, my room was crowded with people. Some were little more than children, some were young adults, and others were even older than I. There was a continuous jumble around my bed—in three languages. Some of my visitors spoke Indonesian, others Chinese, and some English.

They were from all walks of life. One was a three-year-old girl who came with a picture she had drawn for me. She was accompanied by an older sister who had made me a bookmark.

There was also a graying, spidery old Chinese man who would never see seventy-five again. He came with his daughter to visit me. When he saw the black-and-blue marks on my arms he was disturbed.

"That should not be," he said. "I will fix a plaster to take them away."

In the afternoon they were back. He had prepared the plaster and instructed his daughter in how to put them on my arms. Sure enough, they did take away the black-and-blue marks, but that was not what I appreciated the most. It was the kindliness and love behind their action that made the incident so precious.

Some of those who came to visit I had met through the store. Some I had met casually. Four medical students stopped in to see me, with a word of encouragement and several small sponge cakes. I had seen them a number of times and was aware that they were Christians, but I didn't know their names or where they went to church.

The Bible College in Malang sent me a huge bouquet. (I have the feeling they spent far more money on it than they should have.) Chinese friends came with delicacies. One even brought a tin of English biscuits. My room seemed to be filled with all kinds of fruit, the sort of things we would never have bought for ourselves. And one evening during Chinese New Year, two parties came with complete suppers. I had enough to share with the two other ladies in the room.

They marveled at the way people flocked to see me.

"We've never seen anything like this," they said. "You have friends of all ages, both rich and poor, and they all love you very much."

"That is what I meant when I said I had a hundred children," I told them. "It is the fulfillment of God's promise to give me a hundredfold for everything that I have left behind for Him."

The younger woman who was a patient in the bed next to mine had known the Lord as her Savior but had gotten away from Him. I had the opportunity to share Christ with her and she came back to our blessed Savior. We had prayer together several times.

Oh, I almost forgot to tell you that besides all of the above, before I left the hospital a Chinese friend brought me a gift of money that more than paid for all of my hospital and doctors' expenses.

The day I went home I took a taxi to the store; I was going to stop by just for a few minutes to see how things were going. But I got along so well that I dismissed the taxi and stayed at the store the rest of the afternoon.

All my love,
Grace

Chapter 17

Reaching Out

I don't know exactly when or why I began to think of a new field of service. I loved the bookstore in Surabaya, all my co-workers there, and the people we were serving. Somehow I had always felt that my work for the Lord would be completed in that city; that I would retire to the States from there. However, I began to get restive. The work at the bookstore was going smoothly and increasing every year, and I began to feel that God had something else for me in that part of the world. Early in 1967 when I was sixty-seven, He began to lay the islands to the east of Java on my heart.

They say that Indonesia is a land of three thousand islands. Journeying north, east, or west, however, one has to believe it is true. It seems that everywhere one looks, there are islands. Boat travel between the islands is both common and varied. One time you may board a vessel large enough to take Muslim pilgrims to Mecca; the next time you may book passage on an oversize "canoe" with a Johnson motor on the back.

When it comes to traveling by ship in that part of the world, nothing is certain. Shipping companies post notices in prominent places stating the times of arrival and departure of the various ships that ply those waters, but the notices are clearly marked with a plus and a minus sign, which means that the ship may arrive early or leave late. In America such haphazard scheduling would cause an uproar; in Indonesia it is the accepted thing.

In June I decided to travel to the island of Ambon, a thousand miles east of us, and take some literature for the churches there. My steamship ticket informed me that I should be prepared to leave the harbor at 10:00 A.M., June 16. With that in mind, Willard and I went down to the dock and he helped me get my luggage, including five boxes of books and Bibles, on board. I was to be traveling with a Chinese pastor who was returning to his congregation in Ambon City.

This was my first experience journeying by ship between the islands, and I was surprised at the number of people who were traveling on deck. Each one had claimed a little space, room enough to at least stretch out and sleep.

Traveling second class, I was in a four-berth cabin. The pastor had similar accommodations across the passageway. The cabin was nice enough except that the porthole could not be opened, for we were on a lower deck, and the electric fan was not working . . . so it was very hot.

It took me only a few minutes after departure to realize that I could not survive for long in the cabin, so I wandered around the ship. I had previously met a lady from Jakarta who was traveling "deck." As I passed her that afternoon she greeted me and asked me to sit with her.

"Thank you." I sat on the side of her cot. After that I spent most of my time with her during the day, going down to my cabin only to sleep.

I had expected the trip between the islands to be calm and uneventful, but I was mistaken. The wind came up and the sea was boisterous. Going below to eat and sleep was decidedly uncomfortable. For two or three days I ate only some crackers and a little fruit.

"You should have made arrangements to live up here," my new friend said. "You could have rented a cot like I did."

When we reached Makassar, the place where my friend disembarked, I rented her cot for the rest of the trip.

After my first good night's sleep on my camp cot, I woke up at 5 A.M. to see a *hadji* (a pilgrim returned from Mecca) standing, then kneeling—facing toward Mecca as he performed his ritual prayers. All around me were other Muslims and Christians, but no one else prayed publicly. As I saw him, my heart sent up a prayer, "Lord, help me in some way to witness to him without offending him."

After I sat on my cot and read my Bible and had private devotions, one of the young men came over to talk to me. I took out a tract and gave it to him. Others came around and I passed out tracts to them. A few moments later the young man came back again. "Haven't you something longer to read? That's much too brief."

I loaned him my Bible, sorry that I had most of the books and Bibles in the hold. Then I remembered some picture books I had put in my suitcase at the last moment. "Thank you for reminding me, Lord," I whispered.

The young man eagerly took *The Visualized Life of Christ* and read aloud—so all could hear—the Scripture verse under each picture. I saw again the power of the Word of God in literature.

Now, to give more of a picture of this trip, let me quote from a letter I wrote after I returned to Java.

Surabaya
September 29, 1967

Dear Praying Friends:

My heart is overflowing with praise for God's abundant goodness to me on my trip to Ambon. It is now time for a second visit. I have just been down to see the ship, and we should be leaving tomorrow. I have already been on board and ordered a camp cot to be placed in a good spot on deck. I will be traveling with one of the girl Bible students returning from Batu.

While in the "Spice Islands" I learned much of the work of the Lord there, but also saw the indescribable darkness in the lives of some of those who call themselves believers. Many of the Ambonese people are from families that have been Christian in name for over 350 years, but at present know only a life of fear—fear of the power of Satan, fear of others casting sickness or spells upon them. I was familiar with the darkness of heathendom for years in China, but this is far different from anything I saw there. It is a direct Satanic darkness and oppression on those who "have a form of godliness" but know nothing of God's power to deliver and change lives.

There are 998 islands in the Molukus—the group that includes Ambon. I was able to visit Ceram and some of the smaller islands, and I'm longing to get back and visit around some more. There are church buildings all over, but most that I saw were built by the Dutch years ago. There are also some evangelical congregations scattered around the islands, and in almost every instance new and larger church buildings are being built, or extensions being made on the buildings now in use. I had the opportunity to testify and preach in some of them, twice in Chinese and the rest of the time in Indonesian. That was a new experience for me. I had done very little speaking in Indonesian before this trip.

I traveled around by bus, by packet boat, and even by small outboard motorboat. *That* particular trip ended by my crawling over the side of the boat into shallow water and wading ashore. I had my shoes on and one got stuck in the mud. From now on I am going to go Indonesian and take my shoes off.

One trip by mailboat was four hours long. The boat was large enough to hold 150 people (but don't ask how they were all stuffed in) together with all their market-day purchases. There is always space to sit on the roof of the boat. Not that *I* did that! Too much chance of sliding off, for there was no railing. I much preferred to be packed in. At least *in* the boat I was under the roof, away from the sun.

Coming back to Ambon, the packet boat was jammed again, but this time with chickens, bananas—yes, every kind of produce imaginable, as the farmers were taking them to the city for market day.

I had set aside one week in Ambon itself for selling books and Bibles. I arrived with five boxes, and sold the Bibles out almost immediately. In fact, when I left for Makassar (on my return to Surabaya) I had only one box of books left; they were mostly in English, and were actually intended for sale there because of the size of its English-speaking population. Had those books and Bibles been in Indonesian, they would have been long gone.

I arrived in Makassar just after a time of rioting there. I was able to visit the churches and see for myself the damage that had been done. All the benches, chairs and pulpits were smashed and the glass windows broken.

"The Lord has been doing wonderful things in this land," one of the native pastors told me. "Many have turned to Christ. That's the reason the devil is out to hinder the work."

"Praise God, he is a defeated foe," I told him.

"How true that is. After the trouble there were more out to church than ever before."

Trouble and persecution only cause true believers to draw nearer to the Lord. God has a way of working miracles. Remember, we are counting on you to hold us up in prayer, and also the Christians all over this land.

With much love and prayer,
Grace.

Here is another letter I wrote several years later. It tells about one of my bookselling trips on another island—this time Sulawesi.

Manado
August 15, 1969

Dear Praying Friends:

It is long past time that I sat down and wrote to you. Letter writing is one thing I have not done in these months that I have been traveling. I am preparing to go back to Surabaya on the ship sailing the 18th or 19th of this month.

Many times while traveling between towns by boat I have had people ask me to open my suitcase so they could see the books. I have done so and sold right on the spot. While on land I have spread out my books on tables after evening evangelistic services where thousands attended. Other times I have offered my books for sale at English-speaking services where only twenty or thirty attended.

It is pleasing to me to have so many buy books to take to prisons, or to prison camps where political prisoners are kept. There are still thousands in these camps.

In all I have sold five large wooden boxes filled with books and Bibles in this arm of Sulawesi. In addition I have received from Surabaya sixty-five packages of books by mail that weighed eleven pounds each. Besides this I have bought and sold over two hundred Bibles from the Bible Society here, in addition to the five hundred or more indexed Bibles received from Surabaya. I am thankful for all the material that has been sold, but am more thankful for all of the varied opportunities and all of the different places that the literature has gone. Some of my poorest customers were those who left their homes in Bali because of the devastation caused by the volcano and have come to Sulawesi to start life anew.

One of these transmigrants, as we call them, said to me: "The god of our mountain is angry with us. We do not know why, but he showed his anger by spilling fire on our villages and killing many of us. So the rest of us had to leave." There was a hopeless tone to his voice.

"I can tell you about One who loves you," I said. "He will not be angry with you. He gives us real hope and everlasting life!" I gave him a Bible, and his children some picture books. No American child has ever been half so happy with a gift.

"Sowing the seed beside all waters!" What a joy! I would not wish to change places with anyone who only sits in an easy chair.

So many times on this trip it has come to me that Paul preached to others the *unsearchable riches of Christ*. The cry of my own heart is that I may be faithful in first receiving the riches of Christ and then in passing them on to others.

I have a very special prayer request. This year will be the end of my present visa, which must be renewed regularly. But having been here fifteen years, now I can apply for a resident's permit—a permanent visa—which will entitle me to leave and return to Indonesia freely. This means much to me, for it means that a new missionary may then apply for a visa in my place. Anyway, the future is in the Lord's hands, and I am content to leave it there.

All my love,
Grace.

In December I went to the Immigration Office.

"I would like my permanent visa, please," I said to the officer.

Furrows deepened on his forehead. "Is it time?" he asked.

"Oh, yes," I replied. "I came in '54 and this is '69."

He glanced at the records again. "That will be fifteen hundred rupiahs," he told me.

My heart sank. "I thought it was a thousand. I didn't bring any more than that."

"Come back tomorrow with the right amount," he said, "and you can have it."

I was almost afraid to leave his office for fear he would change his mind. (Willard had only been given an extension to his visa the month before.) How I prayed from that moment until the office opened the next morning.

As soon as the office opened I was there with the money and my request for a permanent visa. The official barked an order and one of the secretaries made it out for me. As she handed me that precious visa my fingers were trembling and I was so happy I didn't know whether to shout or cry. Actually, I did neither. I thanked her soberly, and left. But we had a time of praising God in my room that night. It is difficult to explain what that piece of paper meant to me.

* * * * *

Six months after getting my permanent visa I came down with malaria.

Whenever I traveled to a swampy area—like parts of Kalimantan—I would carefully take antimalarial tablets such as Atabrine. On Java, though, there was so little of the disease that I didn't need to take medication. However, I had just returned from a trip to the interior of the island north of us when I came down with a particularly virulent form of malaria.

I was home when I took sick and was almost unconscious when my helper found me. She rushed to the store to tell the Stones. They hurried back to my house, gathered my clothes together and took me to the hospital. Of the next day or two I can remember nothing.

Again I saw a miracle of the goodness of the Lord. I spent three weeks in the best room in the hospital, with two of the best doctors on the island taking care of me. When I asked about my bill, one of the doctors refused to charge me anything. The other doctor, a Catholic, said, "I'm not going to charge you either, but I would like to have an interest in your prayers."

I was charged only for the x-rays, which cost me less than ten dollars.

The last week in the hospital I had some wonderful opportunities for personal witness with the nurses. One, a Bali-Hindu, was particularly hard of heart. But, strangely enough, she liked to come in and sit by my bed in the evening and sing Christian hymns. The night before I was to leave I said to her, "You are going to have to watch out. I am going to pray for you for a year that you will become a Christian."

Another girl I had an opportunity to share Christ with was the one who went to the x-ray room with me. Two days before, someone had given her a booklet which ended with the words "kehidupan yang sempurna" (the perfect life). "Where do you find that?" she asked me. "I want it."

I gave her two books from the store. "You will find the perfect life within these pages. Jesus said, *I am come that they might have life, and that they might have it more abundantly.*" She was so close to receiving Christ that I trust I will see her in Heaven.

* * * * *

When I returned to the States for my furlough and had regained my strength, I talked with Ken Adams about my continuing to serve God in Indonesia, for I was now seventy. The mission, like most, had a policy regarding retirement at the age of sixty-five. But I wanted to stay on as long as my health remained good. They talked things over with Willard, who was still heading up the Indonesian work, and decided God yet had a ministry for me there.

So, at the end of a year's furlough I went back to Indonesia. To me it was "going back home."

Chapter 18

A New Beginning

You can never know how happy I was to be back on the island of Java in the spring of 1972. I am proud of my American heritage, but I could never get used to the furious pace of life on the North American continent. I had lived so long in this part of the Orient, I was geared to a more relaxed, leisurely way of life.

The Christian Literature Crusade gave me permission to remain in Indonesia, but it was decided that I need not be firmly tied to their program. I was to be free to do whatever I wanted to, whenever I wanted to. This, they felt, would be easier for me. I could go at my own pace.

I was concerned about my boat ministry, but didn't know for sure if that was what God wanted; nor had I decided for sure where I should locate. My visa listed Surabaya as my home, but it also gave me permission to live anywhere.

I didn't know where I wanted to live and work, but the Lord moved swiftly. The matter was resolved a week after I got back. Two days after my arrival a pastor from West Irian came to Surabaya and we got acquainted. He asked me to go back with him, and I was so sure it was God's leading that I agreed. So several days after I had reached Java I was boarding a ship with the pastor and a young woman who was also going to West Irian to serve the Lord.

We loaded two truckloads of books to take to that distant island. There were two hundred Bibles and at least one hundred New Testaments, in addition to several thousand books—fourteen huge crates, and a number of smaller boxes and suitcases.

Although West Irian is one of the most primitive islands of Indonesia, there are large cities along the coast that have attracted numerous people from the other islands, including many Chinese.

The ship we were on was large but people were still piled all over the deck. The first night out, the young pastor, Paulus, did not have a place to stretch out and sleep, even on deck, so he lay down in a hallway and hoped nobody would step on him during the night. After our first stop, at Makassar on Sulawesi, it was much better for all of us, for some of the passengers got off and we found a better place to set up the cots and stretch out and sleep.

The ship was going all the way to West Irian, calling at the major ports. We were thankful for that. It meant that we would not have to transfer.

I had the privilege of using my little cassette player as a means of witness. It hardly stopped playing during the entire trip; first one would borrow it and then another. After the hymns had been played many times, we had a song service and everybody enjoyed joining in. I also had five or six copies of *The Life of Christ Visualized.* These were loaned out.

One young man solved a little puzzle card I had given him and came back. "Have you got some more reading?" he inquired.

"I just happen to have something else along," I told him. It didn't take me long to find a copy of one of the Gospels for him and also a good tract that explained the way of salvation.

The trip out was not too enjoyable since we had several hard rain showers. The canvas overhead leaked, so in the middle of the night we had to get up and cover ourselves with plastic to keep dry. When the sun came out, though, it was blistering hot—but we could still have a song in our hearts.

We disembarked at Sorong and I started selling books almost immediately after arriving. I was greatly surprised by the way the stand was received. The sale of books went far beyond our hopes and expectations. The first week we sold to about 150 customers a day.

After two or three weeks, however, sales slowed down to fifteen or sixteen customers a day. I was disturbed by this at first; I began to think that mere curiosity had caused the first surge in sales and now that the people were used to us they were no longer interested. However, I then learned that people are paid by the month. After the tenth of the month all business of any sort drops off noticeably; there are fewer people on the streets and fewer in the markets at night.

What a thrill it was to see the CLC books go out. I was convinced that after the people had read a book and received blessing that they would come back again for other books.

Many of the customers in Sorong had never owned a book before. However, the Christians in the city had been taught that the Bible and song books were important, so there was a firm interest in them already. We sold over three hundred Bibles and New Testaments and were soon waiting for new supplies. One of the pastors told me he could use four hundred song books if they were available.

Wide differences in religious practices were evident in West Irian. Some people practiced a weird mixture of cold, dead Christianity, witchcraft and black magic. Indonesians who had come from southern Sulawesi around Makassar were fanatical Muslims. There were two new mosques in Sorong when we arrived.

After a brief stay in Sorong, I felt led to move to Jayapura, the capital of West Irian. Here, as I had envisaged, we were able to set up a regular bookstore. This has been a place of blessing and encouragement for many people—to national Christians, but also to missionaries. Missionary children would often miss out on Christian books in their own language if it were not for CLC bookshops around the world.

It was my privilege to be "Auntie Grace" to missionaries and nationals alike. One day a missionary brought his four-year-old son into the store to see me.

"I've learned some Bible verses, Auntie Grace," he said proudly. He quoted four or five verses to me, not only saying each verse perfectly but explaining where it was found on the page. When he finished I gave him a Good News Testament as a little reward.

They were still there when an Indonesian father and mother with children came in. Proudly the four-year-old showed the others his New Testament and what he had done to get it.

"Isn't that tremendous?" I asked the youthful Indonesian mother.

"Our children really love the Christian comic books," she said. "They just devour them."

"You know," I replied tapping her on the shoulder, "the greatest blessing a mother can give her children is to tell them Bible stories." I showed her Ken Taylor's Bible storybook in Indonesian. She took that book and bought another.

Although the bookstore work was a rewarding ministry, the Lord gave me an idea for reaching out to others in a less conventional way.

Much of life in the Orient revolves around the street market stalls. In Jayapura there are market stalls that operate into the night hours. To the average American tourist the night market looks and sounds like a completely disorganized mob of people, jostling and yelling for favor with the buyers. It was into this bustling melee of business and humanity that God was leading me.

I began by taking a small table and some of our best-selling books and going down to the market at four o'clock in the afternoon. To my surprise, trade built up and I was eventually selling more at the night market than in the regular bookstore. We were going out where the people were.

I developed a daily routine. Each morning I was up at four-thirty for a time of prayer, after which I went down to the bookstore to supervise that operation. The Lord had given me national helpers. At noon I went home and rested for a few hours. Usually I just lay there—letting God pour new strength into my body. Then I always got up in time to be at the night market when it opened at four o'clock.

We had a few changes of location and eventually settled in a market of three hundred stall holders. Practically all the stall owners were Muslims. Many were fanatical in their beliefs and quite a few of them had made their pilgrimage to Mecca. But I was tolerated.

My customers were from all walks of life. I had not been in the market long when the director of the Protestant division of the Department of Religion came to our stall and asked me to bring a list of books and prices to his office the next day. I didn't understand the reason for his request, but I dutifully went.

"If you can supply all these books at this price, I will give you an order," he said. His order was for three hundred books! The total cost would be $700 U.S. That might not sound like much to an American, but it is a great deal in Indonesian funds. The money had been given by the Indonesian government for Protestant Christian work in literature in the interior of West Irian. The books were to be divided between the various missions and churches working among tribes in what is known as Cannibal Valley. Until quite recently these people had been headhunters.

There was one stipulation on my accepting his order. I had to have the books for him within one month. The books had to be in the mission-operated schools by the time classes would resume! In America a thirty-day time limit on delivery might not be difficult, but I knew ordering such books from Jakarta by mail would be useless! The books came from different suppliers and mails are endlessly slow. We were at the end of the world here!

If I wanted those books on time I had to go after them.

"I'll supply your orders," I said.

Four hours later I was on a ship to Jakarta to get the books. I was able to make a good sale, supply the books on time, and make an important friend at the same time.

Not only that, but on board ship as I returned to Jayapura I met a young Christian Indonesian couple who were to become my helpers.

Marthens and his wife Ruth had been Muslims. He had made a decision for Christ five years before and had wanted to go to Bible School. However his parents had refused to allow him to do so. Then when the "Logos," the Operation Mobilization ship, had been in Manado, Marthens had renewed his vow to serve Christ. I had met this young couple before and it didn't take us long to become reacquainted. Before we reached our destination it was decided that they would stay in Jayapura and help me in the literature work. The Lord has always been so good in giving me national helpers.

Life in Jayapura continued to be eventful. Marthens and Ruth had been living with me for almost a year when one night we were robbed. Our burglar got away with some cheap paperback books, my empty typewriter case and Marthens' glasses. The thief must have been disappointed! However he also took a ring of keys. Surely he intended coming back. We were all nervous after that.

On another occasion, a sneak thief came into our stall at the markets. He grabbed my glasses and dashed off into the crowd. Never one to take such a thing without protest, I shouted as loudly as I could in Indonesian.

"Thief! Thief!"

I started after him. I needed those glasses and had paid too much for them to allow someone to get away with them. Everybody along the row of stalls was alerted. One fellow grabbed an iron hook and clobbered him over the head. I'm glad the hook was small and the blow glancing; I wouldn't have wanted to have seen his skull cracked open! As it was the blow was enough to stop him. One of my friends came running up and grabbed him by the arm.

"I'll take those glasses!" I ordered triumphantly. "And I'm taking *you* to jail."

* * * * *

In August 1973, Ruth was expecting her second baby. She had entered the hospital and after two or three hours a messenger rushed back to the house.

"The doctor wants you to come right away," he told Marthens. "He needs blood for a transfusion."

Marthens went out to find donors with the right type of blood. He was still away when I went to the market as usual.

I had only been open for business a short time, and was sitting at the back of the stall, when suddenly I found I could not speak clearly. About the same time a young man who had helped me sell books at various times stopped by.

"I'm sick," I told him, stumbling thickly over the words. "Can you take over for me?"

He did so gladly.

It was a bewildering situation. My mind was clear. I could remember the prices of all the books and knew whether we had certain titles in stock, but I could not speak plainly. I could not hold anything in my left hand and I could not stand. Yet I did not lose feeling in either my arms or my legs. The young man did not know what to do about closing up and I could not help him, so I sat there, helpless, for almost an hour. I was still sitting behind the table when Marthens came from the hospital.

"I—I've got to see a doctor," I mumbled. "I'm sick."

He closed the stall as quickly as possible and took me to the doctor's office.

"It couldn't have been a stroke," he said. "Your blood pressure and heart are good."

"What was it then?" I asked.

He gave me an answer that didn't satisfy me, so a couple of days later I went to another doctor. After examining me and giving me some medicine he leaned back in his chair.

"You must remember that you are seventy-two years old, you know. You can't do everything the way you did when you were twenty-five! You need to take things easy for a while."

That taught me a very real lesson. I had to realize my limitations.

* * * * *

At least half of the customers in our bookstall are people who do not know Christ. One day a trio of Muslim girls stood before a three-dimensional picture of our Lord and Savior on the cross and studied it curiously.

"Was he a bad man?" one of them asked. "Was that the reason he was nailed to the cross?"

"No," I said. "He was not a bad man. He had never done anything wrong."

"Then why was he treated like that?"

"So He could save us from our sins." I went on to explain the way of salvation.

The Muslims know the power of the printed page. The children in their schools here have been taught since first grade never to accept, touch, or read Christian material. One little child might be interested to look at something, but the child next to him will say, "Don't touch, that's Christian."

But some time ago, a change came about. People here are addicted to movies. Any new film will draw long lines of customers, waiting patiently to buy tickets for the next showing, and usually the films have several sessions from mid-morning till late at night. The movie "Moses" was shown and people from all walks of life went to see it. As Moses was associated with the roots of their own faith, the film caused a change in attitude. Before the film was shown, few of the Islamic faith would stop to look at a Christian book and even fewer would buy one. After the movie, however, small boys would come and buy comic books on the life of Moses.

"Moses! Moses!" they would exclaim gleefully.

Men too will now come in, select a book and move to the back of the stall to read a few pages. And if they don't understand what they are reading, they will ask me to explain it to them. They no longer seem to mind if another Muslim is around.

I have seen Muslims buy the book *Truthfully, Jesus, the Son of God.* I never dreamed that I would see such a thing happen. They are not accepting Christ as I would like to see them, but they are much more open now than in all my twenty-five years in Indonesia.

And I am not quitting yet. As long as I am able to get around and there are people who don't know Christ, I am going to be reaching out to them. I just thank and praise God that I have had the joy of serving Him all these years. I would not change a minute of it, even if I could.

* * * * *

POSTSCRIPT

Grace Chang went to be with Christ on April 10th, 1980, just a few months before her eightieth birthday. She died on the job, early in the morning, at her post in the CLC bookstore. Her last request was that she be buried in the land where she was serving the Lord.

Willard Stone, field leader of the Christian Literature Crusade in Indonesia, said Grace's two favorite slogans characterized her life: "Willing hands" and "Day-by-day grace."

In one of her last letters Grace remarked that maybe the Lord would put the ice cream on her cake by letting her visit China before she died. However, that was not to be. Perhaps the special ice cream on her cake has come in a different way—celebrating eternity with many precious Indonesian and Chinese brothers and sisters in the presence of her Lord.

This book was produced by the Christian Literature Crusade. We hope it has been helpful to you in living the Christian life. CLC is a literature mission with ministry in over 40 countries worldwide. If you would like to know more about us, or are interested in opportunities to serve with a faith mission, we invite you to write to:

Christian Literature Crusade
P.O. Box 1449
Fort Washington, PA 19034